# HOW TO WRITE AN
## ASSIGNMENT

## Visit our How To website at www.howto.co.uk

At **www.howto.co.uk** you can engage in conversation with our authors – all of whom have 'been there and done that' in their specialist fields. You can get access to special offers and additional content but most importantly you will be able to engage with, and become a part of, a wide and growing community of people just like yourself.

At **www.howto.co.uk** you'll be able to talk and share tips with people who have similar interests and are facing similar challenges in their lives. People who, just like you, have the desire to change their lives for the better – be it through moving to a new country, starting a new business, growing their own vegetables, or writing a novel.

At **www.howto.co.uk** you'll find the support and encouragement you need to help make your aspirations a reality.

Visit **www.how-to-write-an-assignment.co.uk**

**How To Books** strives to present authentic, inspiring, practical information in their books. Now, when you buy a title from **How To Books**, you get even more than just words on a page.

# HOW TO WRITE AN
# ASSIGNMENT

## Proven techniques for producing essays, reports and dissertations that succeed

### Pauline Smith

**howto**books

Published by How To Books Ltd,
Spring Hill House,
Spring Hill Road,
Begbroke, Oxford OX5 1RX,
United Kingdom
Tel: (01865) 375794, Fax: (01865) 379ıᴜᴢ
info@howtobooks.co.uk
www.howtobooks.co.uk

Fourth edition 2000
Fifth edition 2002
Reprinted 2003
Reprinted 2004
Reprinted 2005
Sixth edition 2008
Seventh edition 2009
Eighth edition 2011

British Library Cataloguing in Publication Data
A catalogue record for this book is available from the British Library

Consultant editor Roland Seymour

ISBN 978 1 84528 441 1

Produced for How To Books by Deer Park Productions, Tavistock
Typeset by Pantek Arts Ltd, Maidstone, Kent.
Printed and bound in Great Britain by Bell & Bain Ltd, Glasgow

NOTE: The material contained in this book is set out in good faith for general
guidance and no liability can be accepted for loss or expense incurred
as a result of relying in particular circumstances on statements made in the
book. Laws and regulation are complex and liable to change, and readers
should check the current position with the relevant authorities before making
personal arrangements.

# Contents

# List of illustrations

# Preface

This is a practical book explaining how you can really succeed in the skill of writing assignments – essays, reports and dissertations.

Each chapter covers a different stage of assignment writing. Each is illustrated with examples and mini case studies to show you the results of both good and bad practices.

Summary checklists are included to help you, and each chapter ends with self-evaluation questions to ensure that you are on the right lines.

If you read this book and follow the advice and guidance provided, then you should achieve success in assignment writing whether for study, work or pleasure. The skills you acquire should be helpful to you in all sorts of ways throughout your life.

My own students tell me that they have found the book very useful to them and certainly they have produced very good assignments! This eighth edition includes revisions and improvements in order to provide further support for your assignment writing, and includes guidance on online databases and electronic journals to make your research easier. It is used by students across several college and university courses.

When you have read the book I would be pleased to receive any comments and suggestions from you that would be helpful in future editions. Finally, I would like to thank my students and colleagues past and present for providing the inspiration for the case study material and for giving such constructive feedback on the earlier editions.

*Pauline Smith*

# 1 What is an assignment?

Journalists and detectives are asked to take on specific 'assignments' as part of their day-to-day work where they investigate an issue or crime and then produce a report for their newspaper or police bosses. Similarly, students are given **assignments**, by their tutors, as part of their coursework or in preparation for examinations. These assignments are usually in the form of a title question (or **hypothesis**); a short description (or **brief**); or **task**. Students, like journalists and detectives, are expected to investigate or **research** the 'brief' set, and to produce a written piece of work.

An assignment, therefore, involves undertaking both the investigation and the piece of writing which provides evidence of that research. An assignment is both *process* and *product*. This book concentrates on helping you to develop your skills of researching assignments and concentrates especially on how to produce a good assignment.

## Various types of assignment

These are some of the forms that assignments can take:

- essays
- reports
- dissertations.

Let's consider them in turn.

## Essays

These are probably the most popular form of assignment set by tutors for their students on 'A' level to Masters level courses.

Whilst Humanities and Social Science courses are often totally essay-based, some science courses do incorporate other forms of assignment, such as reports (see page 3).

| Essay section | Possible material |
|---|---|
| Introduction | Define any key terms. State what you propose to do in the assignment/your objectives. |
| Main body/ development | Your main points/arguments and supporting evidence/ examples, in a sensible order. |
| Conclusion | A summary of what you have said/argued/discovered so far. A conclusion about how you have fulfilled your objectives. Any recommendations you can make as a result of your work. |

Essays can be set by tutors for both **coursework** and **examination** purposes. Many courses are designed so that a percentage (or even 100%) of the overall marks required for the qualification is awarded for successfully completing a number of coursework essays. The length of these essays varies from course to course but is usually between 1,500–5,000 words each. The final examination is also made up of a number of essays to be completed in a given length of time; three to four essays in three hours is fairly usual.

Being able to write a good essay in a limited amount of time is therefore an important skill to develop!

*Essay structure* – A good essay should incorporate the structure outlined above.

## Reports

This form of assignment is becoming more popular in certain courses, *eg* business and management. Reports have also been used in the writing up of formal research projects in the science area for a long period of time.

| Report section | Possible material |
|---|---|
| Introduction/ aims/objectives | A brief clear statement of the purpose and aims/objectives of the project/activity/investigation. |
| The organisational context | A description of the organisational context and of how the project is influenced by the contextual factors. |
| Implementation | The project/investigation itself; steps undertaken; the evidence gathered. |
| Evaluation | Assessing the extent to which the aims of the project were achieved and the evidence used to make this evaluation. |
| Explanation | A discussion of the factors influencing the success of the project/activity/investigation. |
| Conclusion | A critical reflection on the project with recommendations for future practice. |

A report can be shorter than an essay; it is usually more focused and tightly defined in its structure, using sub-headings suggested by the nature of the research project undertaken.

A report is written to describe and analyse (or assess) what the aims of the project were; what *happened* and *how successful it was* in achieving its aims; and to recommend what *should happen next*.

*Report structure* – A typical project report structure is provided above.

## Dissertations

These are major assignments undertaken towards the end of diploma, first degree, Masters and PhD level courses. Dissertations often count for a large percentage of the overall marks awarded by tutors for the final qualification. For PhD, the dissertation is usually the sole written assignment.

| Dissertation section | Key questions |
|---|---|
| Introduction/research questions/hypothesis | Are the hypothesis or aims clearly stated? |
| Review of literature | Is the review sufficiently extensive? Is the literature reviewed critically? |
| Research design | Is the research methodology adequately justified and is it appropriate? |
| Data collection | Are the issues of validity and reliability considered? |
| Analysis/interpretation | Does the analysis allow the initial aims/research questions to be further explored/redefined? |
| Conclusions/ recommendations | Are the conclusions/recommendations substantiated by the evidence presented? Is there evidence of personal and critical reflection? |

Dissertations can range in length from 8,000 to 25,000 words. The length is stipulated by the examination requirements of the particular course or qualification. For a PhD dissertation, 40,000 to 50,000 words is usual.

*Structure of dissertations* – The structure of a dissertation is usually fairly tightly laid down by the course requirements. Tutorial support is provided to ensure that the final dissertation meets these requirements. The overall structure of the dissertation has similarities with the research project report described above, although the dissertation has clear chapters or sections, rather than sub-sections or headings.

A typical dissertation structure is shown above.

# How your assignment will be assessed

One of the main purposes of setting and writing assignments is for assessment. Tutors set assignments that will allow them to assess a student's

- knowledge
- skills
- understanding

in a particular topic or area of the course. Both coursework and examination assignments are therefore strategies or tools that allow the tutor to assess the student's achievements.

## Understanding the assessment criteria

As a student you really need to understand what tutors are looking for in your assignments – that is the **assignment criteria** used by the tutor to mark your work. By understanding the **assessment criteria** used, you will be able to make sure that your essay, report or dissertation satisfies them – and you will be able to achieve a high mark!

Figure 1 shows a set of assessment criteria (or **indicators** of **achievement**) that tutors on an education degree course use. These are provided openly for the students, together with an explanation of what these criteria mean. Each student can then think carefully about how to provide **evidence of achievement** within their assignment. Even if you are not on an education-related course, spend a few minutes reading these 'criteria' and 'what this means for you' and then answer the questions which follow.

| The criteria | What this means for you |
|---|---|
| 1 Understanding of the theoretical models from which issues and key concepts are derived. | Education is full of **theories**, ideas, models and arguments. Whatever work you are writing about (even practical work), you must link it to the theories and ideas of writers working in this area.<br><br>*For example, if you are asked to describe your ideas about equality you will need to include in your assignment references to the major documents and books on the subject eg The Swann Report 1985; The Sex Discrimination Act; The Race Relations Act 1978; LA Policies on Equality of Opportunity; Equal Opportunities: Gender (G. Hannan 1982); Invisible Women (D. Spencer 1982) etc, etc.*<br><br>You need to show that you understand these key documents and ideas and the way in which they have influenced your ideas (and practices) relating to equality. |
| 2 Link between conceptual framework and practice. | This is easy and very important! It means that you must not simply ***describe*** the theories and ideas of educationalists and writers: instead, you must include examples from your own **practice** to show that you ***understand*** the theories or concepts and can apply this to your own professional experiences.<br><br>*Therefore in relation to equality, you should not simply refer to the LA Equal Opportunities and Multi-cultural or anti-racist policy documents; instead you should show how your own practice, or the practice you observe in the classroom, supports or reflects the theories of equality of opportunity.*<br><br>**BE AS CRITICAL AS YOU CAN!** |

**Fig. I.** Assessment criteria for an assignment.

| The criteria | What this means for you |
|---|---|
| 3 Structural development from objectives to analysis and synthesis, conclusions and recommendations. | The **structure** of your assignment must be very clear:<br><br>(i)  you must set out your **objectives** in the **introduction** – say what you are arguing in the assignment.<br><br>(ii)  in the **main body** of the assignment you should go on to **develop** your argument revealing that you understand the theories,  models and arguments and that you can relate them to your own practical experiences as *critically* as possible.<br><br>(iii) finally, in your *conclusion* refer back to your introduction and objectives and show how you have fulfilled them. If possible make some **recommendations** for teachers/schools to consider as a result of your work. (See also 'Planning and Organising the Assignment'.) |
| 4 Evidence of personal  and professional sell-evaluation. | When you write about the educational practices you have observed, experienced or read about you should try to be evaluative.<br><br>*Look at what you are saying, critically. Is there more than one view or argument or are you simply describing something rather than evaluating whether it is important, relevant, good, bad or could be improved?*<br><br>**BE CRITICAL, BE REFLECTIVE ESPECIALLY ABOUT YOURSELF, YOUR OWN VIEWS AND EXPERIENCES.** |

**Fig. I.** Assessment criteria for an assignment *continued*

| 5  Research activities. | Most assignments will require you to **research**. |
|---|---|
| | *You will need to **investigate** an area of work or study. You will investigate by gathering data or information through: reading relevant literature, using your observation skills, interviewing colleagues and so on. It is important to collect and use as wide a range of evidence or information as possible in order to be able to compare and to interpret what the information is saying.* |
| | **REMEMBER TO BE CRITICAL OF THE DATA OR INFORMATION YOU ARE USING.** |
| | **IS IT TOTALLY RELIABLE?** |
| | **ARE THERE OTHER VALID ARGUMENTS/VIEWS?** |
| 6  Referencing and acknowledgements. | When you refer to a particular author's work, it is important to use the **Harvard system of referencing**. |
| | *With this system you should refer to their name and the date they published their work only, eg 'P. Smith (2010) wrote a guide for students on producing good assignments', but your course tutor will be pleased to talk through these criteria in more detail.* |
| | **PLEASE ASK YOUR TUTORS FOR ANY HELP YOU REQUIRE.** |

**Fig. I.** Assessment criteria for an assignment *continued*

Now examine your *own* assessment criteria. Are they open and shared between the tutor and student? Ask yourself whether you fully understand what your assessment criteria require you to demonstrate in your assignment. If you do not fully understand them (and often these criteria are written in complex assessment language) then you need to ask your tutor for a clearer explanation, so that you can then fulfil their requirements in your essay, report or dissertation.

# Choosing the right format for your assignment

The main purpose of writing an assignment, then, is for you to demonstrate your knowledge, skills and understanding of a particular topic or area of the course to your tutor or assessor. You will be presenting *evidence* of your abilities through the assignment and therefore you need to *consider* its format and structure carefully. Is the piece of work you are producing more suited to the essay or report format?

You may be able to choose whether to write a report or an essay when set the assignment by the tutor. Often the decision is made according to preferred styles of working or old habits gained from our schooldays! Some of us prefer a lengthier, more discursive style of writing, and would probably choose an essay format with its flexibility. Others prefer the tighter and more sharply-focused format of the report.

The aims and title brief of the assignment set by your tutor or examination may, however, determine its format. For example, 'Discuss the advantages and disadvantages of working in a bureaucratic organisation' – this lends itself clearly to an essay format with discursive style and a clear structure. Whereas, 'Evaluate the planning and implementation of a staff development programme in an organisation known to you', lends itself to a report format with its sharp tightly-defined focus; yet, it could also lend itself to a structured essay format – as well as providing the working title for a dissertation!

# Who am I writing the assignment for?

There are clearly overlaps between the essay, report and dissertation in appropriateness of structure. A consideration of the *audience* of your assignment, however, is very useful in determining the overall style and final format. You need to ask, '*Who am I writing this assignment for?*'

In some cases, this audience is clearly defined for you in the assignment brief, *eg* 'Produce a report for your line manager on the effectiveness of the recruitment and selection procedures in operation'. In this example, your audience – your line manager – is clearly defined. You will have a good idea of what is the most suitable type of report (length, style, tone) for this person through your contact with him/her.

Of course your 'other audience' is your tutor/assessor and it is essential that you also have a good idea of what they expect from an appropriate report. Get to know your tutor and the assessment criteria as well as you can. *Find the time to talk to your tutor!* If you are on a distance-learning course, write or telephone. A personal contact will really help you.

In those cases where an audience is not clearly defined in the assignment brief and where your only 'real audience' is your tutor or assessor (and in the case of an examination one you may never have met!), then it is often better to *define your audience* to the reader. At the start of your assignment explain to the reader that you intend to write this essay or report for . . . presentation to your *line manager, future employer, governing body, examiner* and so on . . . In this way you will be justifying the format chosen for the assignment according to the purpose and audience defined by you. You will be in *control* of the assignment from the outset.

---

### Case studies

#### An introduction

In the following chapters we will be following the assignment-writing skills of three different students, Steve, Gill and Sarah. Their individual methods of tackling the various stages in assignment writing will help to illuminate many of the techniques you will need to learn.

#### Steve, a part-time college student

Steve is a young man with a lot of talent on the sporting side. He plays football at semi-professional level; he is relied upon to play cricket for the local team and has just bought a set of golf clubs! Steve works in a garage whilst studying part-time at a Further Education College for two 'A' levels – Biology and Sociology. He needs to pass these 'A' levels in order to gain a place on a PE and Leisure HND course. Steve needs to complete several coursework essays and to prepare for essay writing in the final examination.

### Gill, a management student

Gill is a young woman with ambition. She gained good 'A' level results and has started to work as a management trainee with a large computer manufacturing company. Gill is anxious to gain high level management qualifications to aid her career development. She has registered for a part-time Diploma in Management at the local university. This management course requires students to undertake management research activities and to write several project reports. Gill has never written a management report – her 'A' levels were largely based on prepared essays.

### Sarah, a mature student

Sarah is a mature student. She works full-time as a technology teacher and has responsibility for key stage co-ordination and resources. She had a six year period out of teaching when her children were young and is keen now to develop her career. She has been studying for a part-time MA at the local university, through evening taught courses and independent study. After two years' study Sarah is now doing the final dissertation stage of her degree.

## Summary

- There are various **types** of assignments. Essays, reports and dissertations are three major types used across a wide range of courses.

- Each assignment has a clear **structure**.

- One of the main purposes of assignment is **assessment.**

- It is essential for students to understand the assessment criteria used by the course tutor so that they can provide appropriate evidence of achievement in relation to each criterion.

- The **format** of the assignment may be determined by the aims and title brief given by the tutor, or may be chosen by the student.
- A careful consideration of the audience of the **assignment** can help to clarify the format and structure.

### Self-evaluation

1. (a) What are your experiences of essay, report or dissertation writing?
   (b) How would you define your own present level of assignment-writing skills?
   (c) Which area of assignment writing would you most like to develop?

2. What are the assessment criteria used on your course? Are they shared openly? Do you fully understand them? What types of knowledge, skills and understanding must you demonstrate in your assignment?

3. How do you know whether an essay or a report is the best format? What are the differences and similarities between these two forms of assignment?

4. Who are you writing your next assignment *for*? What is your target audience?

# 2 Making the right start

This chapter asks you to identify those skills and attitudes that will help you to produce a good assignment. You are encouraged to *recognise your strengths* and to identify your preferred ways of learning and effective ways of managing your time. You are also asked to target *areas for further professional development* and to plan how you will achieve those targets.

---

**Warning!** This chapter could change your life.

---

## Finding your preferred style of learning

Writing an essay, report or dissertation is difficult and challenging. It involves a complex learning process. Fortunately, the writing gets easier the more often you practise the skills involved in this learning process. It is also aided by the learner/ writer being more aware of his or her **preferred style of learning** and developing a flexible range of learning strategies.

Considerable research has been carried out over many decades into the processes of effective learning. More recently, the work of D. Kolb and Honey and Mumford has revealed the importance of the student (and teacher!) identifying their preferred learning style and for development programmes to fit **appropriate learning strategies** into their design. In this way, the programme or course will be designed and delivered to suit a range of preferred learning styles within the student group.

## Student-centred and teacher-centred approaches

This **student-centred** approach to teaching and learning has been used in mainstream education and in FE and HE courses to varying extents. How has your course been designed: in a student-centred or teacher-centred way? Examine the descriptors below. Which column most closely matches the design and delivery of your course?

| *Student-centred* | *Teacher-centred* |
| --- | --- |
| Students engage in a variety of activities at any one time. | All students go through the same learning process together. |
| Students control the order and pace of their learning. | Teachers control the order and pace of the programme of work. |
| Students and teachers select jointly from a wide range of teaching/learning strategies. | Relatively few teaching/learning methods are used. They are selected by the teacher according to his/her preference. |
| The teacher is seen as a resource and personal relationships are encouraged. | The teacher is seen as an 'authority' and relationships are formal. |
| Emphasis on a variety of assessment strategies. | Emphasis on the final written examination. |
| Emphasis on the development of practical skills and understanding. | Emphasis on the recall of facts and theoretical knowledge. |

Obviously the above descriptors are stereotypical and most courses will incorporate both descriptors at some point. For example, as the final examination or coursework assignment approaches most students are happy for their teacher to adopt a more teacher-centred and didactic style! Such an approach reinforces the authority of the syllabus and identifies the teacher as the 'source of all wisdom' in passing examinations and gaining qualifications.

Many of us have preferred teaching–learning styles if we think back to our old teachers and those lessons and subjects we enjoyed, compared with those we struggled with. It may be a little unfair to 'blame the teacher' totally for our successes and failures in learning; nevertheless there is a large body of evidence stressing the crucial role of the teacher in the learning process.

Modern teacher-training courses attempt to prepare the teacher in a *wide range of teaching-learning strategies* so that an individual student's preferred learning style can be accommodated flexibly.

▪ Read the *General Descriptors of Learning Styles* provided by Honey and Mumford (1986). Which style – *activist, reflector, theorist* or *pragmatist* – most closely depicts your preferred or usual way of learning?

## Summary of the four learning styles

The learning characteristics of these styles can be summarised as:

---

### Learning Styles – General Descriptors

---

### *Activists*

Activists involve themselves fully and without bias in new experiences. They enjoy the here and now and are happy to be dominated by immediate experiences. They are open-minded, not sceptical, and this tends to make them enthusiastic about anything new. Their philosophy is: 'I'll try anything once'. They tend to act first and consider the consequences afterwards. Their days are filled with activity. They tackle problems by brainstorming. As soon as the excitement from one activity has died down they are busy looking for the next. They tend to thrive on the challenge of new experiences but are bored with implementation and longer term consolidation. They are gregarious people constantly involving themselves with others but, in doing so, they seek to centre all activities around themselves.

## *Reflectors*

Reflectors like to stand back to ponder experiences and observe them from many different perspectives. They collect data, both first hand and from others, and prefer to think about it thoroughly before coming to any conclusion. The thorough collection and analysis of data about experiences and events is what counts so they tend to postpone reaching definitive conclusions for as long as possible. Their philosophy is to be cautious. They are thoughtful people who like to consider all possible angles and implications before making a move. They prefer to take a back seat in meetings and discussions. They enjoy observing other people in action. They listen to others and get the drift of the discussion before making their own points. They tend to adopt a low profile and have a slightly distant, tolerant unruffled air about them. When they act it is part of a wide picture which includes the past as well as the present and others' observations as well as their own.

## *Theorists*

Theorists adapt and integrate observations into complex but logically sound theories. They think problems through in a vertical, step by step logical way. They assimilate disparate facts into coherent theories. They tend to be perfectionists who won't rest easy until things are tidy and fit into a rational scheme. They like to analyse and synthesise. They are keen on basic assumptions, principles, theories models and systems thinking. Their philosophy prizes rationality and logic. 'If it's logical – it's good'. Questions they frequently ask are: 'Does it make sense?' 'How does this fit with that?' 'What are the basic assumptions?' They tend to be detached, analytical and dedicated to rational objectivity rather than anything subjective or ambiguous. Their approach to problems is consistently logical. This is their 'mental set' and they rigidly reject anything that doesn't fit with it. They prefer to maximise certainty and feel uncomfortable with subjective judgements, lateral thinking and anything flippant.

## *Pragmatists*

Pragmatists are keen on trying out ideas, theories and techniques to see if they work in practice. They positively search out new ideas and take the first opportunity to experiment with applications. They are the sort of people who return from management courses brimming with new ideas that they want to try out in practice. They like to get on with things and act quickly and confidently on ideas that attract them. They tend to be impatient with ruminating and open-ended discussions. They are essentially practical, down to earth people who like making practical decisions and solving problems. They respond to problems and opportunities 'as a challenge'. Their philosophy is: 'There is always a better way' and 'If it *works* – it's good'.

Honey and Mumford, 1986.

**Activists**      learn best from the activities where they can engross themselves in immediate tasks (*eg* games and simulations, team exercises, and so on);

**Reflectors**    learn best from activities where they have extensive opportunities to review and reflect on what has happened;

**Theorists**     learn best when what is offered is part of a system, model concept or theory;

**Pragmatists** learn best when there is an obvious link between subject matter and a problem or opportunity on the job.

Each 'style' obviously has its strengths and weaknesses. Research on learning styles can be used to:

- Become more aware of your own 'preferred style'.
- Identify those learning styles which might benefit from further development, thus increasing the effectiveness of a range of learning strategies.
- Develop an action plan to improve and extend the flexibility of your learning styles.

**Strategies** for improving and extending your learning styles include *practising* certain behaviours, skills and attitudes associated with your weaker style.

## Activist style

If you wish to improve your activist style:

- Practise doing something new.
- Change activities each half hour. For example, if you have had half an hour of cerebral activity, switch to doing something utterly routine and mechanical.
- Practise initiating conversations with strangers.
- Force yourself into the limelight, volunteer to chair meetings or give presentations.
- Practise thinking aloud and on your feet. Set yourself a problem and bounce ideas off a colleague.

## Reflector style

If you wish to improve your reflector style:

- Practise observing. Study people's behaviour both verbal and non-verbal.
- Keep a diary; reflect on the day's events and see if you can reach any conclusions.
- Practise reviewing after a meeting or event. Review what happened in great detail. List the lessons learned from this activity.
- Give yourself something to research, requiring pain staking data collection. Spend a few hours in the reference section of the library.
- Practise producing highly polished pieces of writing. Give yourself essays to write on something you have researched. Write a report. Draft a policy statement. When you have

written something, put it aside for a week then force yourself to return to it and do a substantial rewrite.

■ Practise drawing up lists for and against a particular course of action or issue. Whenever you are with people who want to rush into action, caution them to consider alternatives and to anticipate the consequences.

## Theorist style

If you wish to improve your theorist style:

■ Read something 'heavy' and thought-provoking for at least 30 minutes each day. Try to summarise in your own words what you have read.

■ Practise spotting inconsistencies/weaknesses in other people's arguments. Take two newspapers of different persuasions and do a comparative analysis.

■ Take a complex situation and analyse why it developed the way it did. Do a detailed analysis of how you spend your time.

■ Collect other people's theories, hypotheses and explanations about events. Try to understand the underlying assumptions each theory is based upon. See if you can group similar theories together.

■ Practise structuring situations so that they are orderly. Try structuring a meeting by having a clear purpose, an agenda and a planned beginning, middle and end.

■ Practise asking probing questions – the sort of questions that get to the bottom of things. Ask questions to find out precisely why something has occurred.

## Pragmatist style

If you wish to improve your pragmatist style:

■ Collect techniques, *ie*: practical ways of doing this, for example time-saving techniques; presentation techniques and so on.

- Concentrate on producing action plans. Never emerge from a meeting or discussion without a list of specific actions with deadlines.

- Study techniques that other people use and model yourself on them.

- Get experts to observe your technique and to coach you in how to improve it.

- Tackle a 'do-it-yourself' project at home or work – *eg* learn to type.

Source: Honey and Mumford (1986).

## Drawing on all four learning styles

It can clearly be seen that there are behaviours, skills and attitudes in all four learning styles that are appropriate to writing a good assignment.

For example: thinking aloud and on your feet (activist); giving yourself something to research and write and rewrite (reflector); analysing in detail what happened (theorist); and using experts to coach you in a particular technique (pragmatist) are all valuable components of successful assignment production.

### Ask yourself

- What personal strengths can you identify in your preferred learning styles?

- What areas have you targeted for further development?

## Managing your time effectively

One of the techniques the **pragmatist** would see as valuable in assignment writing is **time management**. The following section helps you to practise the skills or techniques of managing your time more effectively in both your 'everyday life' and in your 'studying and assignment writing life'.

Most part-time students, like those in our case studies, will be suffering from 'overload' and 'deadlines'. They will find it difficult to devote sufficient time to the assignment researching and writing process. It is, of course, essential to see assignment writing as a high priority, planned activity, and allocate quality time to the whole process.

The following time management techniques and strategies are designed to help you to make effective use of the short amount of time you have available to you. Practising time management should prevent procrastination and a lack of preparation and planning. Your assignments will be submitted on time and your stress levels will be reduced!

## 1. Recording your use of time

Keep a time log or diary and record all of your activities (preferably for one week). See Figure 2.

| TIME LOG | |
|---|---|
| DATE: _____ | |
| **TIME** | **ACTIVITIES** |
| 08.00 | |
| 08.15 | |
| 08.30 | |
| 08.45 | |
| 09.00 | |
| 09.15 | |
| 09.30 | |
| 09.45 | |
| 10.00 | |
| 10.15 | |
| and so on | |

**Fig. 2** A time log

## 2. Analysing your use of time

Consider how your time is spent. Have you wasted time – how? Is your time too *fragmented*? Could you *consolidate* small parcels of free (or relatively free) time into larger more useful units of time by moving or reviewing activities? Do *unplanned* activities tend to take over from *planned* intentions? Why?

### Ask yourself:

(a) What am I currently doing with my time?

_____

(b) What actually needs doing?

_____

(c) How much priority do I attach to the remaining tasks?

_____

(d) How can I achieve more?

_____

| Time management – action planner | | | | | |
|---|---|---|---|---|---|
| Things to do | (A) Must do | (B) Should do | (C) Could do | Delegate to whom? | Achieve by when? |
| | | | | | |

**Fig. 3** Time management: action planner.

# 3. Improving your time management

Consider the following techniques, questions and strategies and ask yourself whether these are a strength for you or an area for further development.

■ *Clarify objectives*
Are you clear about your objectives? What are your long-term objectives? Why do you want to pass this course/write this assignment? Are you clear about the objectives for the assignment? (See Chapter 3.)

■ *Planning*
Effective planning saves considerable time overall. Always plan your assignment carefully (see Chapter 4). Use a daily 'to do' list, a diary and a long-term planner to carry out forward planning for the day, week, year. See Figure 3.

■ *Prioritise*
Prioritise your activities into categories of:

(a) What you *must* do.

(b) What you *should* do.

(c) What you *could* do.

■ *Delegate*
Can you delegate any of the above tasks and responsibilities to other colleagues? Have you involved your colleagues or tutor sufficiently in the task/assignment?

■ *Say 'No'*
Analyse why you say 'yes' when you know you should say 'no'. By saying 'yes' you are probably putting additional pressure on your short supply of time. Learn to be more assertive; practise four steps in saying 'no': listen; say no; give reason if appropriate; suggest alternatives if possible.

■ *Dealing with paperwork*
Learn to speed or skim read documents; adopt an effective system of classifying and storing the information you will be

gathering; learn to use IT – word processing and database can save time in information handling.

- *Eliminate time wasters*
  These include the telephone and other unplanned activities and temptations. When you are working on your assignment be focused; do not be side tracked.

- *Identify your best hours*
  Do you work more effectively in the mornings, after-noons, evenings or in the night? Use your *quality* time most productively.

- *Effective meetings*
  These include course meetings and tutorials. Decide if the meeting needs to be held/attended; decide on the purpose and outcomes of the meeting; decide on the starting and finishing time and stick to these times; make sure you partici-pate effectively in these meetings to achieve your aims.

You may wish to study how to manage your time in more depth. The work of J. Adair (2004) and P. Drucker (1995) are both val-uable sources of time management strategies for the busy assignment writer to consider.

---

## Case studies

### Steve the activist

Steve is an *activist*. He likes variety and excitement, works quickly and gets others involved and enthusiastic. He works well with other people and talks readily to strangers both on and off the sports field. In his 'A' level classes he is not concerned with making a fool of himself and will ask questions and volunteer opinions readily. His major strengths are his ability to ask for help and to talk through any problems in his essay writing with his tutor and colleagues.

Steve is, however, a fairly typical activist in that he has a tendency to rush into essays without careful planning and he is not very good at *managing his time*. He leaves things to the last minute and tries to do too many things at once instead of prioritising his limited time.

**Gill the theorist**

Gill is a *theorist*. She has set herself clear goals in obtaining her management diploma and has *prioritised her time* in pursuit of this goal. She has always worked well alone with minimum help from teachers and colleagues. Gill is precise and thorough; she organises her facts and material and plans well in advance for her projects and reports. Gill likes to work things out clearly on paper and also to rework her notes over and over again.

As a theorist used to drafting and redrafting 'A' level essays, Gill may find it difficult to adapt to report writing. She has a tendency to fail to use teachers and colleagues as a resource and can get bogged down in information and theory. At the moment Gill does not function very well in group discussions and active learning situations, preferring the more didactive style of teaching she is used to.

**Sarah the reflector**

Sarah is a *reflector*. She is unhurried and doesn't get into a flap. Sarah's strength lies in her ability to listen to others and share ideas. She is good at pinpointing important new questions, coming up with new ways of doing things; and in presenting her work in interesting and appealing ways. As a reflector she can see the long-term implications of things and has chosen a long course (the MA) which will allow her to study several different subjects.

Sarah is, however, a fairly typical reflector in that she sometimes doesn't see the 'trees for the wood' and forgets important details. She is also a little uncritical of ideas, too easy-going and not assertive enough with teachers or friends. Sarah's time management skills also need to be examined. She waits too long before getting started; doesn't like planned time tables; only works in bursts of energy and can get easily distracted from the job in hand. Sarah has a 20,000 word dissertation to write this year.

# Summary

- It is important to start from where you are now; to recognise your strengths and skills and to identify and target areas requiring further professional development.

- Recognising your *professional learning* style and its relative strengths and weaknesses is important in developing a flexible range of learning styles and strategies useful in assignment writing.

- *Time management* can be an effective strategy in assignment writing, ensuring adequate preparation, planning and prioritisation of the work involved. Effective time management can help to reduce the stress levels of the busy assignment writer.

## Self-evaluation

1. What learning styles should our case studies aim to develop in order to improve their assignment writing? What is your preferred learning style? What skills do you intend to practise from the other learning styles?

2. Which teaching-learning strategies have you experienced recently? (See page 27)

3. Is it important for tutors to incorporate a wide range of teaching-learning strategies into their course design and delivery? Why?

4. Keep a time log for one week and analyse your use of time. Consider the time management strategies and analyse your targets for further development. Action-plan those targets by practising the relevant techniques and skills. Do you need any help? Reflect and critically evaluate over the period of one term whether you have made more effective use of your time.

| Teaching/learning strategy | Tick |
|---|---|
| Games | |
| Role play | |
| Brainstorming | |
| Case studies | |
| Debates | |
| Individual work | |
| Whole group teaching | |
| Working in groups | |
| Syndicates | |
| Demonstrations | |
| Surveys | |
| Interviews | |
| Tasks/challenges | |
| Design briefs | |
| Computer assisted learning | |
| Video/film | |
| Work experience | |
| Field studies | |
| Lectures | |

# Notes

# 3 Analysing the title question or brief

The title question, or brief, of your assignment is very important. It tells you and the reader what is going to happen in the assignment.

You need to read your title question or assignment brief very carefully, several times! In the case of an essay or a brief for a report, you need to decide **what you are being asked to do** before you can even start to plan. In the case of a dissertation where you select your own title and research question, you still need the same close matching of response to question in order to ensure relevance and coherence.

It is important to practise the skills of **analysing questions, titles and briefs** in order to fully understand what is expected of you – so that you can then respond with a relevant and pertinent assignment. This section helps you to analyse key words and ideas in the title question or brief of essays, reports or dissertations.

## Identifying the key words

You need to examine the precise wording of the title question or brief in order to establish what this particular assignment (and the tutor) is looking for in terms of **evidence** of achievement. The title question or brief will carry, within its words, its own **assessment criteria** – that is, the important concepts, knowledge and skills you are required to include in your assignment to satisfy the criteria already established.

Chapter 1 outlined the importance of understanding the assessment criteria your tutor will be using to judge your assignment. Analysing the key words in the title will help you to clarify the criteria relating to both **content** and **process**. See Figure 4.

| Process words: a key to their meanings | |
|---|---|
| *Key word* | *Meaning* |
| Account | Account 'for' asks you to give reasons for. An account 'of' asks for a detailed description. |
| Analyse | Make a detailed examination or investigation into something. |
| Assess | Consider in a balanced way the points for and against something. |
| Comment | State clearly your opinions on the topic in question. Support your views with evidence. |
| Compare | Look for the similarities and differences. |
| Contrast | Emphasise the differences between two or more things. |
| Criticise | Give your considered opinion about the value of the theories/ practices, back up your criticism with evidence from your research (reading, observation, and so on). |
| Define | Give the precise meaning of something. Show how the distinctions you make are necessary. |
| Describe | Give a detailed account. |
| Discuss | Investigate or examine by argument; give reasons for and against. |
| Evaluate | Make a judgement about the value/importance/worth of something. |
| Examine | Present in depth and investigate fully the implications. |
| Explain | Make plain, interpret, give reasons. |
| Extent | 'To what extent' – asks you to weigh the evidence for and against something: to state 'how far' something is valid. |
| Illustrate | Use examples, diagrams and so on to explain or make clear. |
| Interpret | Make clear the meaning of something, usually giving your own views also. |
| Justify | Show adequate grounds for decisions or conclusions. |
| Outline | Give the main features, structure or general principles of a topic omitting minor details. |
| Review | Make a survey of; critically examine the subject. |
| State | Specify fully and clearly. |
| Summarise | Give a concise account of the main points of the topic. |

**Fig. 4** Process words: a key to their meanings.

## Three steps to take

Try following these three steps in analysing the key words in title question or brief:

1. First, look for the **process** word – discuss, plan, review, evaluate, and so on. The sort of words (usually verbs) tells you *how* you must deal with the content of the assignment. Underline these key process words and check their meaning (see below).
2. Next, look for and underline the **content** words – social class, leadership style, The Children Act 2004, and so on. These words tell you what you *must* focus on in the assignment.
3. Finally, read and write out the **whole title question** or brief, trying to establish precisely what you are being asked to do. What is the content area? What must you do with that content? What sort of structure, style and audience is indicated?

---

**Tip** If you are in any doubt at all about the meaning of the assignment brief, seek advice from your tutor or experienced colleague.

---

## Techniques for understanding the instructions

When you have underlined your key content and process words (and read the question through several times!) you will have some **general idea** of what you are being asked to do. You will know whether the topic requires a general or specific treatment. You will know whether you can include your own opinions and experiences, or whether you should include only the views or theories of other writers.

You need to analyse the title question or brief very closely and the following techniques may be of some further help:

- using a dictionary
- rewriting the question in your own words
- looking at the opposite view
- recognising the type of question.

Let's consider each in turn.

## Using a dictionary

**Use a dictionary to check the meaning of every individual word.** Even *ordinary* words like 'should' or 'must' need to be 'unpacked' and defined by you.

Take for example the question 'To what extent should parents prepare their children for school?' This requires you to explore the key **content** words of 'parent', 'children', 'school' and 'preparation'. It also gives you the key **process** words 'to what extent' asking you to state 'how much preparation' parents should make. But what about the word 'should'? If you look in the dictionary 'should' is defined in terms of 'duty' or 'obligation'. This will immediately give you a good critical idea for your assignment in that you can explore the whole questionable notion that parents 'ought to' prepare their children for school. Should they? Why is it a *duty*? – and so on.

## Rewriting the question in your own words

Translate the whole question into your own words. Try to avoid using any of the same wording as in the title question or brief. You will probably find that your translation will be double the length of the original question. No matter! – it will help you to fully understand the point or emphasis of the question.

If you have any difficulty in translating the question into your own words the dictionary will help. Also, *Roget's Thesaurus* can be most helpful in finding synonyms, partner words and different forms of the same content or process word. This translation and redefinition should really help you in the next stages of assignment writing.

# The opposite view

**Try writing down the opposite of the title question or brief.**
This technique can often provide illuminating ideas about how to
tackle the question and raises interesting arguments not always
considered.

For example the previous question could be rephrased: 'To what
extent should parents not prepare their children for school?'
is critically raised for you to consider as a possible line of
argument.

# Recognising the type of question

**Make sure you recognise the type of question being asked
– and therefore the type of assignment in style, structure,
format.**

This technique requires you to examine the process words
carefully (see above). For example 'discuss' tends to depict an
open-ended question – where if you are not careful you could
discuss far too widely! A useful  technique is to define the limitations of your discussion in your opening paragraph, *eg* 'In this
argument I intend to discuss the following important factors . . . in
the space available, I do not intend to discuss the relative merits
of . . . although it is recognised that such factors also play an influ-
ential role in . . .' and so on. In an open-ended assignment, you
need to define your 'limitations' or 'restrictions of focus' clearly
to the reader.   In this way you will be assessed on what you have
justified as important and included in the assignment, and not on
what you have left out.

Other types of questions can be categorised as descriptive,
analytical or argumentative. Again, study the 'process' word to
decide what you are being asked to do.

## *Descriptive assignments*

These tend to be structured in a chronological or survey/review
of literature fashion. They are often difficult to write well in a short
assignment and many students end up writing too much!

## *Analytical assignments*

These allow the structure to be determined by the writer, according to the categories, sub-sections, factors chosen for the analysis. Analytical essays are usually well-organised as long as you tell your reader how you are going to proceed with the analysis at the beginning of the assignment.

## *Argumentative assignments*

These allow the topic to be the subject of critical debate, setting out arguments for and against the issue under investigation. Differing and competing viewpoints are used to structure the assignment and the writer needs to understand these different arguments and to use them effectively.

---

- Essay questions can require you to be descriptive, analytical or argumentative.
- Report briefs can require you to be descriptive and/or analytical.
- Dissertations can require you to be descriptive, analytical and argumentative.

---

### Case studies

#### Steve is asked to 'critically discuss'

Steve has a sociology essay to submit by Monday evening entitled: '*The essential functions of the family in Britain are in decline. Critically discuss this statement.*' He has left the essay to the last minute unfortunately, and has arranged to play football on both Saturday and Sunday afternoon. Steve knows that he needs to get a good mark on this essay and has read quickly around the area of the functions of the family. On Friday evening he is ready to write the essay and he rushes straight in.

Steve has not analysed closely the title of the essay. In his haste, he failed to spot the key words 'essential' and 'critically' and instead writes a descriptive essay which supports the statement that the functions of the family in Britain *are* in decline without giving any opposing arguments – *eg* around the area of 'essential'.

When his assignment is returned, Steve realises that he failed to answer the question completely – he is determined to analyse the question closely next time!

## Gill is asked to 'assess'

Gill has been asked to produce a report to *'Assess the effectiveness of the departmental resource allocation system operating in your organisation'*. She needs to hand it in to her tutor on Monday. In her precise and thorough way she has spent considerable time reading widely in the area of resource management; she has assembled many facts and theories on effective resource allocation, from an extensive range of management text books. By Friday, she too has left the writing of the report a little too late, still getting bogged down in theory after theory.

Gill has identified the key words 'effective' and 'resource allocation'. However, she has failed to appreciate the importance of the process word 'assess', in relation to considering the strengths and weaknesses of her own particular system at work. Gill needs to apply her theories to practice. Analysing more closely the word 'assess' would have helped her to consider in a balanced way the effectiveness of her own system; it would have alerted her to the need to give her own judgements, rather than simply those of lots of theorists!

## Sarah's 'investigation'

Sarah has her second tutorial with her dissertation supervisor on Monday after school. She has decided that she would like to do some research into teacher stress and National Curriculum testing. After much creative thought on the way to the university, Sarah suggests the following title for her dissertation to her tutor:

*'A study of the National Curriculum and an assessment of its impact on teacher morale and pupil achievement.'*

Sarah's tutor helps her to focus down on what she really wants to do in her research. 'National Curriculum tests (SATS)' and 'teacher stress' are identified as key content words and the tutor suggests that Sarah will be 'investigating' rather than 'assessing'. This results in the working title of: *'An investigation into the relationship between teacher stress and National Curriculum testing'*. A good starting point!

# Summary

- Understanding the title question or brief is very important in answering the right question.

- Analysing the **key words** will help you to define the important concepts, knowledge and skills you should include in your assignment.

- Look for and underline **process** and **content** words.

- Use a **dictionary** to check meanings.

- **Translate** the question into your own words. Use *Roget's Thesaurus* to find helpful synonyms.

- Try writing down the **opposite** question to see if it sparks new ideas.

- Learn to recognise the **type** of question being asked (open-ended, descriptive, analytical, argumentative) and therefore the style and structure of the answer.

## Self-evaluation

1. Look back at your previous assignments and tutor comments. Have you ever misunderstood the point of what is being asked for in the question? Have you ever failed to fully understand the emphasis of the question? Did you analyse in detail the key words in the question?

2. Identify the content and process words in the following title question:

   'Evaluate the extent to which an understanding of equal opportunities helps to inform recruitment and selection practices.'

   Your answer probably included 'Equal Opportunities' and 'recruitment and selection' as key *content* words and 'evaluate', 'extent' and 'inform' as key *process* words.

3. Translate the above title question into your own words. Use a dictionary and *Roget's Thesaurus* to find as many meanings and interpretations of all the words as you can.

# 4 How to plan and take notes

Before you can start writing you need to create a *plan* for your assignment. This is usually best done in three steps:

1. **Brainstorming** every idea and piece of material you think you might include; and using **patterned notes** if possible.
2. **Making notes** on relevant material in the area; **collecting further information**. Note: Online databases and electronic journals available in your library make it easier for you to find out what has been written on the topic.
3. Drawing up an **outline plan** of the assignment with a clear structure and a logical order.

This section will help you to develop the essential skills of the pre-writing stage – brainstorming, note-taking and outline planning.

## Brainstorming

The last chapter asked you to analyse 'key words'. If you were to analyse 'brainstorming' using the dictionary, you might question the value of having a 'violent mental disturbance' (*Oxford Dictionary*) to effective assignment writing!

However, after analysing the title question or brief, many people do find it helpful to brainstorm the subject or topic concerned in order to generate ideas and material for their answer. Try the following brainstorming activity yourself:

## Example

Take a sheet of blank paper and write in the middle of it the subject or questions to be considered. Then write down *everything* that comes into your mind which is connected with the subject or question. It does not matter at this stage about the order of the things you write down. You can include trivial and even loosely associated thoughts since these might trigger an interesting line of argument. Write in note form, quickly. Give your thoughts a chance to flow freely and creatively.

You could draw a **spider** or **bubble diagram** if you wish – see Figure 5.

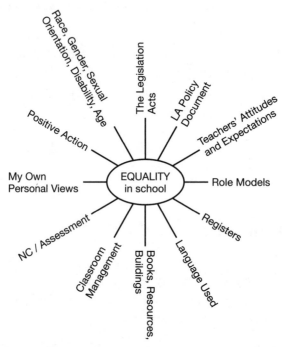

**Fig. 5** Example of a spider diagram

A further variation on brainstorming which takes you one stage further towards detailed note-taking is a technique called **patterned notes**. The Open University Open Teaching Toolkit describes how this style of note-taking can be used.

The title/main idea/topic is written in a box or bubble in the centre of a plain sheet of paper (*eg* A4 turned sideways). Then themes are written along lines radiating out from the centre and subsidiary points branch off from these main branches. Dotted lines/arrows can be added to bring out links and connections between points. You can use different coloured pens to highlight main points and so on. See Figure 6.

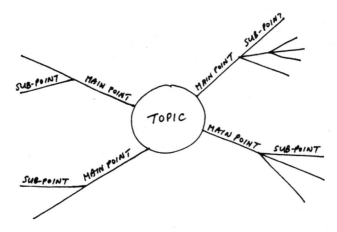

**Fig. 6** Example of a patterned note.

*Source*: Open University 1992.

## Note-taking and collecting further information

After analysing the title question, brainstorming, and using patterned notes to identify what you already know or questions you would like to pursue on the topic or subject, it is time to *gather further information*. This information in the form of notes will come from a variety of relevant *sources eg*:

books

films

video

radio programmes

periodicals

encyclopaedias

abstracts

indexes

talking to other people

online databases

electronic journals

Online databases and electronic journals in your library can save you time and make it easier for you to find out what has already been written on the topic you are researching.

## Coping with a flood of new ideas

As you collect information from your sources you will find yourself asking new questions and having new ideas and arguments to include in your assignment. You will therefore be modifying and improving your earlier brainstormed or patterned notes through a careful collection of relevant information. *You need to take care to collect enough information and not to collect too much so that you get bogged down in notes and detail!*

## Noting useful examples

As you read your books and articles, watch TV, listen to radio programmes and delve into the reference section and online facilities of the library it is *important* to keep a note of all useful examples, illustrations, definitions, quotations and references, as well as possible points of argument.

## Keeping the right type of notes

The *type* of notes you keep will probably vary according to the subject and the type of source you are using (interview, textbook, TV, programme, article). You can write your notes on *separate sheets of paper* or *cards* so that you can shuffle them around when it comes to the detailed planning and writing stage of your assignment. It is important to remember to keep a *record and web address of the source* of your note (the author, title, publisher, date of publication). This can save you hours of time searching for that particular book or article you know you copied a quotation from.

Using IT, for example a personal computer, can prove helpful in storing and retrieving data or notes made during this stage of assignment writing. You will develop your own style of note-taking (to suit your preferred style of learning, perhaps!).

Some people tend to keep highly organised records or notes whilst others are a little more disorganised or impulsive. Experience will help you to find a style of note-taking that is effective for you.

## Producing an outline plan

Planning your essay, report or dissertation makes effective use of your limited time. By preparing a plan you put yourself in control of the material you have collected and you will be able to present your assignment in a logical, concise and coherent way.

---

**Tip**  Remember, in examinations, drawing up an outline plan of what you intend to include in your answer is valuable for the examiner to see. It could gain you marks!

---

The basic framework of the essay, report and dissertation is provided in Chapter 1 and the paragraph, sub-heading and chapter heading forms the major organisational device giving structure to the assignment.

---

**Tip**  Try writing an assignment without any paragraphs or headings at all to see how completely disorganised it looks!

---

At the outline planning stage you should aim to organise your *selected notes* (*ie* those items you have decided are relevant to the title question or brief) into a logical order in order to create a clear structure. You should ensure that your assignment plan uses all of the relevant ideas and material you brainstormed and collected earlier. You should also ensure that the whole assignment plan is designed to answer the title question or brief set!

There are various planning techniques to use in assignment writing from simple *lists* under *key headings*, to *planning trees* and a detailed form of **patterned notes**. The use of these methods will vary according to personal preference and to the formation or structure of the assignment. However, the planning tree and patterned notes could be useful for planning an essay, report and the literature review chapter of your dissertation. Figure 7 is an example of patterned notes and Figure 8 an example of a planning tree.

Whatever planning method you decide to use, the end result must be an outline plan that is **systematic** and **organised**. The material must be **logically ordered** and the paragraphs and/or sub-sections **clearly indicated** as above.

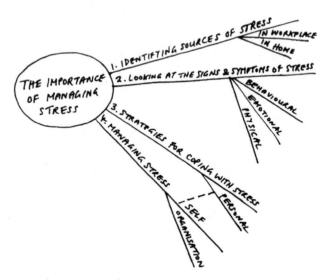

**Fig. 7** A patterned note on managing stress.

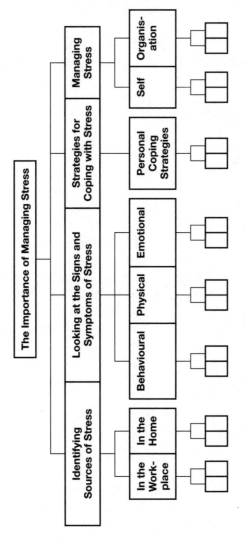

**Fig. 8** Example of a planning tree on managing stress.

## Case studies

### The typical activist's approach

Steve is a typical activist in that at the moment he does not plan his work well in advance. He leaves things to the last minute instead of planning an effective use of his limited time. Steve is good at brainstorming ideas to include in his assignment; but in his last sociology essay he failed to organise these ideas into a logical structure that answered the question set. His tutor, realising Steve's inexperience in essay writing, has loaned him a book on planning techniques. Steve is willing to try any new ideas or techniques and is going to use the planning tree next time!

### Gill the theorist

Gill is a typical theorist in that she plans well in advance for her assignments. Indeed, she spends hour after hour gathering detailed information in the library using the online facilities and making copious notes. Her notes are so detailed that she found it difficult to organise them all into her last report. Gill would benefit from going through a more creative stage before delving into detailed note-taking. After analysing the brief for her next report she should consider brainstorming all possible lines of enquiry; she should then use patterned notes to select the important and relevant ideas and concepts or questions requiring further exploration in the library. This technique may help to reduce the amount of information Gill gathers, helping her to get down to writing the report earlier and to valuing her own opinion and viewpoint.

### Sarah's energetic and creative approach

Sarah has managed to successfully complete several short assignments in her MA pathway, over the last two years. She has a tendency to work rather sporadically and with bursts of energy. Like a true reflector, Sarah is good at coming up with creative solutions to assignment questions or problems to be solved. She is also easily able to identify important questions which must be considered. Sarah has long used the brainstorming technique to generate ideas for her assignments, but her tutor's comments reveal that she has often failed to organise and use her excellent ideas effectively in a logical and coherent structure, to answer the question set. Adopting detailed planning techniques, such as a planning tree or patterned notes, will ensure that in future Sarah capitalises on her powers of reflection and does not forget to include important details or material in her dissertation.

# Summary

- Brainstorming the title question, subject or topic can help to generate ideas and material for the answer.

- Using **patterned notes** can help to take the state of ideas generated one stage further and raise questions for further exploration.

- Collecting relevant information for the assignment can be helped by developing an effective style of **note-taking**.

- Producing an **outline plan** of your assignment with a logical order and clear structure is essential. **Planning trees** and **patterned notes** can help in this outline planning stage.

## Self-evaluation

1. Look back at a recent assignment. Does it have a clear structure? How did you plan the structure of the assignment?

2. Try brainstorming what you know already about 'writing a good assignment'. Can you extend these brainstormed notes into patterned notes with main points and sub-points?

3. Practise using both a planning tree and detailed patterned notes in your next two assignments. Which technique is most helpful to you in defining the structure of the paragraphs and sub-sections?

# Notes

After producing an outline plan (see Chapter 4) the next stage is the writing of a **rough draft** of your assignment. In this stage you will try to keep to your plan, but expressing your ideas clearly often means that you come up with new and better ideas as you write. This can involve you in restructuring your original plan, but these revisions will probably be minor ones!

As you write your rough draft you will be using **paragraphs** and also **sub-headings** and **chapter** headings. These organising devices help to clarify the structure of your assignment to the reader and **signpost** your main and supporting (sub) points.

This section takes you through the **skills of paragraph writing** and emphasises the importance of writing good **introductory** and **concluding** paragraphs, sections or chapters.

## Paragraph writing

### One point per paragraph

Each of the main points in your outline plan needs to have one or more paragraphs devoted to it. In other words a paragraph should cover only one idea or key point. If a main point has several supporting (sub) points then these key points will probably each require a paragraph.

In the example given on page 48 it would be wrong to put physical, behavioural and emotional signs of stress into one paragraph since each is a *different* sub-point of the main point. Therefore each sub-point deserves a separate paragraph and there is also a considerable amount of information to include on each of these aspects of stress (see Figure 9). Indeed, as you write you may find yourself further sub-dividing your points into further paragraphs in order to keep the paragraphs a reasonable length.

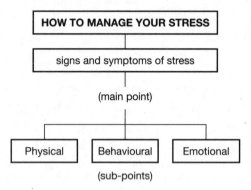

**Fig. 9** Structuring your assignment into paragraphs. Each sub-point will probably require a separate paragraph.

## A paragraph can vary in length!

A paragraph might occasionally consist of just one sentence (usually to give maximum effect to the key point you are making). An average paragraph is probably around 100 words and no longer than half a page in length. If your essay, report or chapter needs to be about 2,000 words long then you can quickly check your outline plan to see if you are attempting to 'fit in' too many main and sub-points, or whether you might need to add further sub-points through additional research if necessary.

## How many paragraphs?

Look back at the planning tree on page 43 and decide *how many* paragraphs should be included in this assignment on 'How to manage your stress'. Don't forget to include an introduction and conclusion. What might be the *approximate length* of this assignment, as indicated by the main and sub-points included in the plan?

# Highlighting key points

The one **key point** in your paragraph needs to stand out clearly to the reader. This key point is placed in a **key sentence** usually at the start of the paragraph, so that you are then explaining to the reader what this paragraph is about. Therefore the first sentence in any paragraph is usually very important as it summarises the main or sub-points covered in the paragraph. (Each of the other sentences in the paragraph should go on to explain or illustrate the key points that the paragraph is making.)

■ What is the main or key point of the paragraph above? Is there a key sentence? Where is it placed?

*Note:* Although key points are usually made at the beginning of paragraphs they can also be made in the final sentences of paragraphs!

■ What might be the advantage of this technique?

# Joining it all together

Paragraphs need to be **coherent**, which means that the sentences must link with one another. If each sentence in the paragraph is discussing or further exploring the same key points then the paragraph will probably be coherent. However, it can help to use **transitional words** to join your sentences together and to make the paragraph flow more smoothly.

Examples of transitional words include 'for example', 'on the other hand', 'however', 'similarly', 'in contrast', 'therefore', 'for instance', 'furthermore', 'in other words' and so on (see page 57).

■ Look back at the preceding paragraphs and identify the transitional words used to add coherence and linkage within the paragraphs.

Using transitions to link your sentences helps you to write more clearly and also helps the reader to understand the key points you are making and extending. Transitions can also be used to link paragraphs together effectively (see Chapter 6). Paragraphs are important in *all* assignments, whether essays, reports or dissertations. They give structure and order to the piece of work. However, they are not the only organisational devices or *signposts* that writers can use.

## Using sub-headings

The sub-heading can be used as a structuring signpost for the reader not simply in reports or within dissertation chapters, but they can also be used effectively in traditional essay writing. Sub-headings are deliberately obvious and point out clearly to the reader the main point or argument being explored in the subsequent paragraph(s). This ensures that the reader (or examiner!) fully understands the point(s) you are making.

Using sub-headings in a humanities or social science essay can be very useful. They provide **structure** and a set of **signposts** for the reader to follow through often very detailed descriptive, analytical or argumentative essays. Sub-headings, therefore, help to inform and guide the reader.

- Look back through this book to see how sub-headings are used as signposts to guide the reader through the material on assignment writing.

## Writing introductions and conclusions

### Introductions

An introduction can act as a major signpost in the assignment. This is the first opportunity for you to direct and guide your reader, giving them a clear idea of what is to follow.

The following points will be useful in ensuring that your introductions are effective.

*Note:* introductions should:

- **Define** the key words and ideas to be used in the essay, report or dissertation. Avoid long-winded definitions.

- Explain clearly how you have **interpreted** the question or brief. What you understand by the title.

- State which **aspects** of the topic you intend dealing with and why. Justify your selected **focus**.

- Say **how** you intend to tackle the question: the **structure** and **order** of your essay, report or dissertation.

- Aim to be bright, crisp and make the reader want to read on. No more than half a page in length, preferably less.

In a **dissertation** or **report** you will need to state the hypothesis and/or research question(s) you are going to investigate and then to report on.

In an *essay* it is useful to pose a question in the introduction which you will then pursue through the main body of the essay.

## Example 1

*'In this report/dissertation I intend to investigate the potential relationship between effective teams and leadership style.'* My research questions will include: What is an effective team? What is leadership? What is meant by leadership style? What are the perceptions of the research group on the potential relationship between effective teams and leadership style?

## Example 2

*'Social class differences in Britain are disappearing. We are all middle-class now. Critically discuss this statement.'* This essay might start with a question to grab the interest of the reader and to identify a line of argument you intend to pursue. For example: 'With three million unemployed and many thousands homeless, how can we claim that Britain is undergoing a process of embourgeoisement?' The introduction might then go on to identify those social class differences of wealth, income, occupation, education, status and so on that would be explored in the main body of the essay.

## Writing conclusions

A **conclusion** is very important as these are the last words you leave with the reader or examiner. Both first and last impressions are vitally important!

The following points will be useful in ensuring that your conclusions are effective.

*Note:* conclusions should:

- pull the assignment together
- answer the title question or brief set
- summarise the main points you have covered
- indicate areas for further research
- include your own personal views on the topic
- not end abruptly in case the reader feels you have run out of words
- end on a crisp and pertinent point which illustrates your main arguments and findings.

In conclusion to this chapter, please remember that all writing is hard! Producing a draft of your assignment that you will be happy with first time is unlikely. You will need to work on your paragraphs, sections, introduction and conclusion by drafting and redrafting them.

- *Writing is a skill. It takes time and practice to develop.*

---

**Case studies**

### Steve – good flow, poor structure

Steve enjoys writing freely – just as it comes! He decided against producing a rough draft in his last sociology essay on 'the family' due to a shortage of time and he wrote the finished version straight off. His largely descriptive essay flowed easily but the structure was not made clear to the reader in the introduction. Steve did not analyse the title question closely and did not define the terms and ideas critically at the beginning of the assignment. Some of his paragraphs were overlong and his conclusion ended abruptly. Steve failed to summarise the points he had made in the essay. In a follow-up tutorial, Steve's tutor encouraged him to clarify the structure of his essay more clearly to the reader in the introduction; to use sub-headings and to use the conclusion to pull the essay together. Steve learns quickly by talking things through with people and he is certain to take these techniques on board next time!

### Gill – clear structure, weak follow-through

Gill likes to set clear goals in her life and in her assignments. In the introduction to her recent report she clearly identified the main points of 'effective resource allocation' which she was about to cover, and clarified the structure of the report. She used sub-headings to signpost the important theories she covered and in her conclusion she summarised the theories of 'effectiveness' and 'resource management'. However, she failed to link the two concepts together sufficiently in a practical assignment. Neither did she add her own personal views. The report was well structured and precise in its theoretical detail, but it was descriptive rather than analytical, and rather bland.

### Sarah – getting at what the title means

Sarah has been asked to produce a rough draft of her introduction to the dissertation for her next tutorial. In it she needs to 'unpack' the working title to clarify her hypothesis (her belief that there is a relationship between teacher stress and national curriculum assessment). Sarah needs to define her key terms. She also needs to identify her research questions (what specific questions will she be pursuing in this investigation?). The rough draft introduction to the dissertation is a most important planning or signposting tool for the rest of the research. Clarifying her objectives at an early stage in the research will help Sarah to focus down and will make the data collection stage more manageable. Sarah is good at seeing the 'total picture' of teacher stress but is finding it difficult to focus down on specific research questions. Her tutor is happy to guide her in this area and Sarah leaves the tutorial session having pinpointed several key questions.

# Summary

- **Paragraphs**, **sub-headings** and **chapters** are useful ways of **structuring** and **signposting** your assignment.

- Each **main** or **sub-point** should have its own **paragraph**.

- Paragraphs need to be **coherent**. Using **transitional** words can help to link sentences and make paragraphs flow.

- The **key sentence** in the paragraph explains to the reader what the paragraph is about.

- **Sub-headings** proide structure and signposts for the reader and are useful in essays, reports and dissertations.

- **Introductions** are major signposts. They should define the key words and state clearly what is going to happen in the assignment.

- **Conclusions** need to pull the assignment together and sum-marise the main points covered.

## Self-evaluation

1. Pick up a periodical in the library and examine one or two articles. What are the main structuring devices used by the author to signpost the material in the article? Is the structure clear? Do the signposts help to indicate the main points or arguments?

2. Analyse a series of paragraphs. What is the topic of the paragraph? What is the main point? Where is the key sentence placed? What is the approximate length of these paragraphs?

3. Read three or four introductions and conclusions to these articles or any essays, reports, dissertations you can obtain. Analyse how clearly the introduction defines the topic and states clearly what is going to happen in the piece of writing. Analyse the effectiveness of the conclusion in terms of pulling the writing together and in summarising the main points covered.

# 6 Improving your style

So far we have **analysed** the title question and **planned** and structured the paragraphs and sections to produce a **rough draft** of the assignment. When you have finished writing your rough draft you have completed most of the *hard* work on your assignment. Drafts, however, need to be redrafted – perhaps more than once in order to get the assignment right! At this redrafting stage you will be **editing** your work. This chapter helps you to edit in order to improve your overall **style** of writing and to check your **punctuation**.

Remember! Nobody finds assignment writing easy – it always involves hard work and a rejection of some of your earlier ideas and writing in favour of better ones.

## Working with a rough draft

Wherever possible write a rough draft, work on it and then leave it for a few days before you write the final draft. Leaving the assignment for a few days will allow you to review it a little more objectively. Alternatively, you might ask a colleague or tutor to read it and comment on it. You may want to change a sentence or paragraph; re-arrange the order or add something important you have missed out. Either way, *give yourself time to reflect on your whole assignment* before you sit down to produce your final draft.

## Achieving the right 'tone'

Check the **tone** of your assignment. Have you pictured your audience and written in a manner appropriate to them? If you are in doubt about the **level** of writing to aim at, then imagine that you are writing for an intelligent 'lay person' – someone who is interested in your subject but who knows little about it. This will stop you *assuming* that your reader understands what you mean, when you actually need to define your interpretation. When you make general statements, always support them with reasons or examples. Too much use of 'I think' or 'I feel that' can have the effect of making the assignment too personal or subjective in its tone. In a formal essay, report or dissertation a casual 'chatty' or conversational tone is inappropriate.

## Terms to avoid

Avoid using **slang** or 'fashionable' terms such as 'cool' or unnecessary 'jargon' – use your own words instead. You should also avoid using **abbreviations** such as 'e.g.' or **acronyms** such as 'TV'. Instead, you should write these terms out in full: 'for example' and 'television'. The use of **contractions** such as 'can't', 'haven't', 'don't' should not be used in formal assignments although they may appear within direct quotations (see Chapter 7). Instead, you should write out the words in full: 'cannot', 'have not', 'do not'.

## Keeping it clear and simple

Write in a **simple and straightforward** language. Generally stick to short sentences; avoid long complex sentences with several clauses where the reader might lose the point. A 'good style' is clear and concise so that the reader can follow your argument or analysis easily and they are not distracted by 'flowery', 'pompous' or 'over-embellished' writing. Set out your arguments clearly in your own terms and avoid adding irrelevant detail or 'padding'.

## Avoiding plagiarism

Do not **plagiarise**. This occurs if you use another author's words without acknowledgement and it can seriously affect the assessment of your assignment. You should always give **references** for any 'direct quotation' from another author (see also Chapter 7).

You should also *acknowledge the original source* of any words or ideas which you use in your own words, *eg* 'It is possible to define management as a combination of both art and science and to agree with J. Humphries (1992) that it also requires "a large helping of common sense"'.

Do try to use your own words as far as possible. An assignment that is full of quotations and references can sometimes appear disjointed and lacking in your own interpretations. It is often best to **paraphrase** – *ie* to express another person's thoughts in your own words and to acknowledge their source.

## Keeping it flowing

Help your assignment to flow by using **transitions** (see also Chapter 5). Transitions are words or phases which help you to write clearer assignments that are more easily understood by the reader. Using transitions to link both sentences and paragraphs together adds to the coherence, continuity and style of your written work. Figure 10 gives examples of some common 'linking' words or phrases and what they can be used for.

| Transition words and phrases ||
|---|---|
| **Purposes** | **Common linking words and phrases** |
| To extend an argument or point you could use | In addition; similarly; furthermore; moreover; also . . . |
| To contrast two points you could use | Whereas it can be argued that; however; on the other hand; in contrast; yet; nevertheless; on the contrary . . . |
| To illustrate an argument or give examples of a particular point you could use | For example; for instance; that is; in particular; in this case . . . |
| To conclude a topic, section or the whole assignment you could use | To conclude; to summarise; to sum up; in conclusion; in brief; as a result; therefore . . . |

**Fig. 10** Examples of transition (linking) words and phrases.

# Avoiding gender and other bias

Watch for gender bias in your writing. Try to use **non-sexist** language at all times. Do not use 'he' or 'his' when you are referring to both sexes. Instead use 'she or he'; or 'he or she' or 's/he'. If this makes your sentence clumsy you could change it to include a 'pronoun' or use the plural. For example, instead of 'the student and his assignment' you might be able to use 'students and their assignments'. Instead of 'the reader . . . he is able' you might be able to use 'readers . . . they are able'. Advice to Open University students in writing their assignments includes the principle that males should not always be placed first in order. It is better to alternate the order, *eg* 'women and men'; 'her or his'; but do not mix your orders in the same sentence or paragraphs as it may sound awkward (Open University 1993).

---

**Case study**

### Steve improves his planning

Steve has taken on board the tutor's advice regarding analysing the title critically. Using a planning tree he has structured the paragraphs for his next sociology essay on *'The differences between males and females in British society are diminishing. Discuss.'*(See Figure 11.)

The first section of Steve's essay is included on page 62. It can be seen by his planning tree that he has now addressed the structuring of his essay well. However, he must ensure that his work does not become compartmentalised and disjointed. Steve needs to use transitional words and phrases to protect the 'flow' of his essay. If he had allowed 'time' to reflect on his rough draft (even overnight!) instead of writing it all up on Sunday evening then he would have noted and addressed this problem of linkage. Steve has never really thought about gender bias until his study of the 'Sociology of Sex and Gender'. He is now trying to use non-sexist language in all his essays. Has he succeeded?

### Gill works on structure and tone

Gill is working on her third draft of the report to senior management on 'The Effectiveness of Mentors within the Staff Development

---

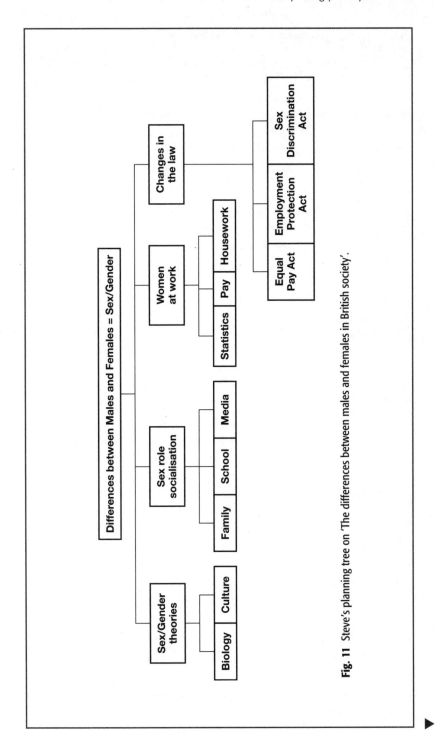

**Fig. 11** Steve's planning tree on 'The differences between males and females in British society'.

Programme'. She has analysed the title brief well and has taken on board her previous weaknesses with regards to applying the theories to practice. She has therefore carried out some research in her own organisation into mentoring and has interviewed several colleagues on their views of its effectiveness. She has structured all of the sections and paragraphs of the report well and has now written them up to her satisfaction. Gill puts this third draft to one side for a couple of days before finally word processing the report and handing it in to her course tutor.

When she returns to read the draft she finds that she is still happy with the analysis, structure and application of the theories to practice and she thinks the findings are very useful and pertinent. However, she is unsure about the 'tone' of the report. At the moment it is written totally for her senior management and there are many specialist terms and acronyms throughout the report. These terms are used commonly in her company but they would mean little to her  course tutor. She decided to write out all acronyms in full and to define any specialist terms to the reader at the beginning of the report. A good move!

**Sarah's handling of sources**

Sarah is now three months into her MA dissertation. She is happy with her title and research questions and has been busy in the university library using the online catalogues and indexes to gain interesting sources and references on 'Teacher Stress' and 'National Curriculum Assessment'. With an array of notes taken and an awareness of the danger of a lack of structure, Sarah has sought additional tutorial support to help her to plan the 'literature review' better with clear sub-headings that reflect her major research questions. She found that this 'plan' helped her considerably and she was able to organise her notes (on separate pages) under each of the planned sub-headings. Sarah has now produced her draft of the literature review chapter and is about to share it  with her tutor.

Sarah's tutor is pleased with the structure of the chapter. It is clear that Sarah has done a lot of research into the relevant literature using the university library online databases and electronic journals. However, the tutor is concerned to see that, although Sarah does reference correctly when she quotes directly from another author's work, she has also written large chunks of the 'sources, signs and symptoms of stress' sub-section without acknowledging the work of key stress management theorists in these areas, even though she has used several of their ideas in her narrative. Sarah did not fully realise the seriousness of not acknowledging the source of her ideas in terms of 'plagiarism'. Also, she did not realise that her work would benefit academically from the inclusion of more references to the research she carried out in the library over many hours.

## Summary

- Give yourself **time to reflect** on your drafted assignment. Put it to one side for a few days and then reread it.

- Check the **tone** of your assignment. Write at an appropriate level for your audience, or write for an intelligent lay reader. Do not allow the tone to be too 'conversational'.

- Check that you have not used any **slang** terms, **abbreviations**, **acronyms** or **contractions**.

- Make sure that you use **simple** and **straightforward** language. Present clear and concise points and arguments in your own terms.

- Do not **plagiarise**. Instead paraphrase another person's thoughts into your own words and acknowledge their source. Reference all direct quotations used and the sources of your ideas. (See Chapter 7.)

- Help your assignment to 'flow' by using **transitions** between paragraphs and sentences.

- Watch for **gender bias** in your writing. Always use non-sexist language.

▶

## Self-evaluation

1. Ask yourself whether you are giving yourself enough time to produce the assignment. Do you deliberately put your draft essay, report or the chapter of *your* dissertation on one side for a few days and then return to it afresh to review it initially? Do you use a colleague as a critical reader? Is your tutor willing to give you feedback on your draft assignment before final marking? Have you asked her/him?

2. Analyse this chapter (or the book as a whole) in terms of simple and straightforward language. The author has tried to be clear and concise in style and has tried to avoid 'over-embellished' writing. Has she succeeded? Can you follow the points easily?

3. Read the three paragraphs of Steve's next essay below and consider *transitions* and *gender bias*. In what ways might it be improved?

Some anthropologists argue that the biological or genetic differences between males and females are responsible for the differences in life style between men and women in society. Males are more aggressive and stronger by nature than females and it is right and proper that they should undertake most of the work in society and also take the dominant position of power.

It is claimed that women are programmed to produce and care for children and are most suited to less strenuous tasks in society and to carrying out work in the home. Since mothers bear and nurse children they automatically have a closer and stronger relationship with them than anyone else. One of these writers, J. Bowlby, argues that 'a mother's place is in the home', caring for her child especially during his early years. He argues that if a mother and child are separated in the early years, it can cause the child to be psychologically disturbed.

There are major differences in brain structures between males and females. Males have a superior right-hand side of the brain giving them more highly developed spatial skills; whereas females have a stronger left-hand side of the brain which gives them superior skills in language. Adapted from: Bowes, Gleeson and Smith (1990).

## Comment

Did you suggest that a transitional phrase such as 'on the other hand' at the start of the second paragraph; and 'whereas, another group of sociologists argue that . . . ' at the start of the third paragraph would improve the flow of writing? You may have found the need for other transitional words, *eg* between sentences, in order to improve the flow of the writing.

Should Steve have reversed 'males and females' in the first paragraph? You might have decided that this would be useful considering the fact that this is a sex and gender sociology essay. (But remember to alternate such terms in a science, maths, management or engineering assignment, also!) Did you spot the penultimate sentence in the second paragraph where the child is male? It would be preferable to use the 'plural' – *ie* 'children' and 'their', rather than indicate to the reader that all children are male.

**Notes**

# 7 Presenting your final assignment

This chapter explains how to use the conventions of

- quotations
- references
- bibliographies
- appendices
- summaries and abstracts

to help you to present your assignment in a correct and appropriate form. It also outlines important aspects of **layout** and **presentation** in your written or typescript final copy. Let's consider each of these in turn.

## Using quotations

Quotations are useful in **illustrating** or **supporting** a point you are making in your assignment. You will be quoting from someone else's work and it is important to check that your quotations are accurate.

A quotation needs to be clearly indicated to the reader as being 'a quotation'. There are conventional ways of presenting quotations so that the reader knows which words are yours and which belong to another author.

### Using shorter quotations

If the quote is *short* then it will fit into your own text and is simply indicated by quotation marks or inverted commas (a single inverted comma is usual).

*Example* – First impressions count in presenting assignments to your tutor and the same is true in writing for publication where a 'sloppy manuscript won't get a warm welcome' (C. McCallum, 1999).

## Using longer quotations

If the quote is *longer* than two lines then it is better to set it apart from your own words by:

- using a colon to introduce the quote to the reader;
- adding a space above and below the quotation;
- indenting the quotation; and
- using single line spacing when the rest of the assignment is double line spaced.

*Example* – In her book *The Beginner's Guide to Getting Published* Chriss McCallum (2008) supports the argument that first impressions count and says that:

> 'Your submission says a lot about **you**. When you give an editor a crisp, clean, well set-out manuscript, with accurate spelling, grammar and punctuation, you encourage him to have confidence in its content, even before he reads it.'

## Quoting part of a sentence

Finally, if you are quoting only part of a sentence, to fit into your own words and to maintain the flow of writing, then you need to indicate that some of the author's words are missing by the use of **dots**.

*Example* – First impressions count in presenting assignments to your tutors or a manuscript to your editor. The important point is that you 'care about what you're doing, and that... you're approaching the job in a professional way'.

# Providing references

References provide the **source** of the quotation or paraphrase you have used and are important in preventing possible plagiarism (see Chapter 6). Out of interest, the reader may wish to pursue a source further and you must therefore make sure that your reference is accurate and detailed.

There are two basic ways of handling references:

- footnotes
- Harvard referencing.

## Using footnotes

Basically footnotes work by inserting small **superscript** numbers into your text which then guide the reader to the note which is provided by you at the bottom of the page, end of chapter or end of the dissertation (sometimes referred to as end-notes).

*Example* – 'Your submission says a lot about *you*. When you give an editor a crisp, clean, well set-out manuscript. . .'. [1]

- See footnote at the bottom of this page.

You will see that the footnote contains all the detail the reader would need to pursue the particular source, *ie* the name of the author, the title of the publication (underlined or italic), the name of the publisher, the date of the publication and the page number of the quote or point.

Footnotes are useful since the reader can usually see the source of the quote or acknowledgement very quickly without turning the page. However, footnotes can take up a lot of room on the page and the numbering system can be a little inflexible and difficult to alter. If you are using the same source several times over you

---

[1] Chriss McCallum, *The Beginner's Guide to Getting Published*, 6th edn (How To Books 2008) p.39.

can, however, shorten the footnote to the author's surname and the page number (once you have written out the reference in full the first time it is used): *eg* McCallum, p.39.

*Abbreviations in footnotes* – Some writers still use the abbreviations 'ibid.' (meaning 'the same') and 'op.cit.' (meaning 'the work cited') as part of their referencing systems. When an author's name is referred to more than once then these forms of short-hand can help. For example, if you are referring to an author's work consecutively then you could use 'ibid.' in the footnote or end-note. So, 'ibid. p.45' could be used instead of McCallum, p.45. Similarly, if you are referring to an author's work that you have already quoted before (but not immediately before) then you could use 'op.cit.' in the footnote or end-note. For example, 'Humphries, op.cit., p.12' could be used in this book because the work of John Humphries was referred to in Chapter 6.

■  Warning: this system of footnoting can be difficult and cumbersome. It is difficult to know how much space to leave at the bottom of a page and if you use 'ibid.' or 'op.cit.' the reader may still be flicking through pages to find the full reference!

## Using Harvard referencing

The Harvard system of referencing does not entail numbered quotes and footnotes. Instead you include the **author's name** and the **date of the publication** in brackets in your text. The reader then looks up the reference in your list of references or bibliography. If you are referring to quotes or a specific item you also need to include the page number.

Harvard systems are easier to write and to change, but they can tend to interrupt your text more, especially if you are referring to several authors or sources. You need, therefore, to work on 'the flow' of the writing (see Chapter 6).

The Harvard system is now generally used in many universities, for example the Open University, in preference to the use of 'footnotes'.

*Examples* – The first reference given in this chapter used the Harvard system of referencing. Here is a paraphrased version where the author's name appears within the sentence rather than at the end:

> For example: In relation to presentation, C. McCallum (1999) argues that an untidy manuscript will not be well received by the publisher.

You will have noted that in the first Harvard reference (see page 66), where the author's name appears at the *end* of the point or paragraph the *whole* of the author's name and date was placed in brackets. Whereas, when the reference to the author's name is included as *part of* your own text then only the *publication date* will be placed in brackets.

## Preparing bibliographies

You must list the references of all your quotations and sources of information in full at the end of your assignment. These references must be arranged alphabetically by the author's surname. It may, therefore, pay you to keep your references as you write in a separate electronic document; or on separate cards or pieces of paper so that you can quickly order them for the bibliography.

Some courses and particularly dissertations require you to separate your *types* of sources (books, articles, Internet, electronic journal articles, oral information, and so on) into sub-sections of the bibliography. The sources within each sub-section will then be arranged alphabetically. You will need to obtain from your tutor a copy of the course referencing procedures, since it is possible that each course within the same university or college may vary slightly in its requirements.

## The accepted format for a bibliography

The examples of bibliographic format given below are generally well accepted throughout the academic world. As a basic rule you need to be sure to include the following details for each reference:

- The author's name (surname, initial of given names)
- The date of the publication (in brackets)
- The title of the article (in single inverted commas)
- The title of the book (or journal or newspaper) italicised (and volume and editions and page numbers)
- The publisher's name
- The place of publication.

## Examples: books

*(a) Single author:*

Evans, M. (2002) *Exams are easy when you know how*, How To Books, Oxford.

*(b) Two authors:*

Smithers, A. and Robinson, P. (2006) *Physics in schools and universities, 11: patterns and policies*, University of Buckingham, Buckingham.

*(c) More than two authors:*

Black, P., Harrison, C., Marshall, B. and William, D. (2003) *Assessment for learning: putting it into practice*, Open University Press, Maidenhead.

*(d) An author's chapter in an edited book:*

Grundy, S. and Robinson, J. (2004) Teacher professional development: themes and trends in the recent Australian experience, in: C. Day and J. Sachs (Eds) *International handbook on the CPD of teachers*, Open University Press, Maidenhead.

■ *Note:* the book and not the chapter is italicised.

*(e) If a book has more than one edition:*

Make clear in the bibliography or list of references which edition you have used:

Smith, P. (2009, 7th edn) *Writing an Assignment*, How To Books, Oxford.

## Examples: articles in journals, periodicals, newspapers

(a) Journal

Gleeson, D., Davies, J. and Wheeler, E. (2005) On the making and taking of professionalism in the further education workplace, *British Journal of Sociology Education*, 26 (4), 445–460.

■ *Note:* the journal and not the article is italicised and you should provide the volume number, the edition number and page numbers.

(b) Newspaper

Whitston, K. (2008) Working for social mobility, *the Education Guardian*, 16th September 2008, p.10.

■ *Note:* the newspaper is italicised and not the article.

## Example: oral information

State whether it was a lecture, conference, television or radio programme:

(a) Staley, J. (2005) *Teaching assistants and the school workforce of tomorrow* conference, Institute of Education, London, 13th July.

## Example: Internet sources and electronic journal articles

(a) For the *Internet*: be sure to put 'online' after the title of the document and where the information is available from. In square brackets supply the date you accessed the site:

*Eg:*

Standler, R. (2000) Plagiarism in college in the USA. Available online at www.rb2.com/plag.htm [accessed 22 September 2008].

(b) For *electronic journal articles*: the same rules apply – give surname, initial of given names, year of publication (in brackets), title of article (enclosed in single inverted commas), name of journal underlined or in italic, the volume and issue number of the journal, the available online information and in square brackets the date you accessed the site.

*Eg:*

Song, K. and Catapano, S. (2006) 'Improving literacy skills with urban children in USA: seeing themselves in literature books', *International Journal of Learning*, 13(3), 111–118, available online at: http://ijl.cgpublisher.com/product/pub.30/prod.1021 [accessed 22 September 2008].

## Preparing appendices

An appendix is a section at the back of the assignment, after the bibliography, where you can include **supporting data** to corroborate your findings. It is particularly useful in a report or dissertation where detailed material relating to the data collection stage can be placed more appropriately in an appendix; placing it in the main body of the assignment would make it appear cumbersome and inhibit the flow of your points and arguments.

You must remember to *refer* to your appendix in your text and you need to *number* and *title* each appendix to match up with the references in the body of the report or dissertation.

## Example

*Appendix 1* provides a complete list of the brainstormed *sources of stress* generated by those Key Stage 2 teachers included in the sample.

Remember to include your appendices in the list of contents at the front of your assignment.

# Compiling summaries or abstracts

An abstract is a summary or **synopsis** of the completed report or dissertation. Obviously it can be written only when you have completed your report or dissertation; and you should spend time on doing it well. An abstract gives a clear picture of the main structure, approach and findings of your report or dissertation to the reader in no more than 200 words. It is important to do full justice to your research and often these abstracts are included in library catalogues, indexes and journals.

# Successful layout and presentation

After all your hard work in writing the assignment it would be a great pity if its assessment by the reader was affected by a poor presentation. Most assignments are word processed these days. If you need to hand write it, make sure your handwriting is neat and legible.

## Techniques to help you

The following points will be helpful in terms of producing an acceptable layout and overall presentation (see also Figure 12):

- Wordprocess/write your assignment on A4 sized paper (this is the standard size these days, but some foolscap is still around). A4 measures 297 × 210 mm.

- Leave a wide margin (at least 4 cm) on the **left-hand side** of the page for your tutor to comment fully.

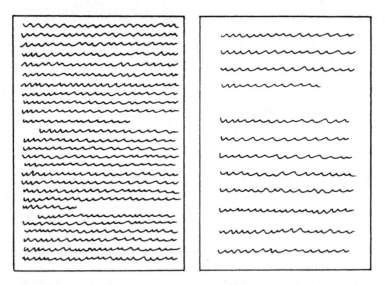

Single-line spaced, with little or no margin.

Too crowded – no space for tutor's comments.

Double-line spaced, wide margins top, bottom, left and right.

An easy-to-read layout with wide margins 'framing' the writing.

**Fig. 12** Examples of good and bad page layout for an assignment.

- Your **right-hand margin** does not need to be quite as wide, but do not write/type to the edge of the page. A 'justified' right-hand margin looks neat (as in most of this book).

- Leave wide margins (4 cm) at the **top and bottom** of each page. This may seem a lot, but it does 'frame' your work and enhance its appearance (see Figure 12).

- Try to learn how to **type** or **word process** your work – it improves the presentation greatly. If this is not possible write as clearly and neatly as you can in *black* ink.

- Leave a **double line space** between your sentences, except where quoting which should be indented and single line spaced.

- Triple line space between **paragraphs** so that you do not need to indent the first word.

- Write/type on one **side** of the paper only.

- If your word processor has a **spell check** facility – use it.

- Always provide a **cover sheet** giving your name, the assignment title, course title, tutor's name and date.

- To help your reader understand the structure of the assignment provide a **contents page**. This is normal in dissertations but is also useful in essays and reports.

- Keep a **photocopy** of your assignment in case it gets lost.

- When posting your assignment to your tutor use a large envelope. **Do not fold** your assignment.

- Tutors prefer to mark assignments which are presented as in example two in Figure 12. They are easier on the eye and **allow more space** for tutor comments.

## Case studies

### Steve's handwriting problem

Steve has been working hard on improving the structure and style of his 'A' level essays. Both of his tutors are pleased with his development over the last term and a half; the future looks promising in terms of continuing development and increasingly high grades. However, Steve has noticed that both tutors underline words and put question marks in the margin as if they could not fully understand his point. When Steve saw his tutors and asked about the question marks, he was told that some words were difficult to read.

One tutor asked Steve whether he could possibly word process his work and pointed out that the college library had several computers available for such a task. Steve decides to improve his handwriting immediately! He leaves more time for the writing up stage, improving his layout with wide margins at the top, bottom and sides and he writes clearly in black ink. Steve has also enrolled for a short word-processing evening course – even though it will mean arriving later at his regular Thursday night rugby club meeting.

### Gill struggles with references

Gill has been working hard on her mini-project reports throughout the last two terms. She is now engaged on her major 5,000 word

▶

management project report entitled 'Effective team leadership in the Personnel Department'.

Gill has been meticulous in referencing every quotation and source that she had used in her research and she has now accumulated a long list of references for her bibliography. Unfortunately these references are not in alphabetical order, and Gill has to spend an hour writing them out in order that the office secretary who has volunteered to type Gill's report can copy them accurately. Next time Gill vows to use a card index system that can easily be sorted, or better still use a personal computer.

Gill is using an appendix to the report to include supporting material such as: 'The Staffing Structure of the Personnel Department'. She has referred to this appendix in her report through a numbering system, for example Appendix 1, and she has given the appendix a title. Unfortunately, Gill has omitted to include the appendices in her 'List of Contents' page at the front of the report.

### Sarah puts the finishing touches

Sarah has been working hard on her dissertation and has now referenced and acknowledged fully the work of the other researchers working in the field of teacher stress and National Curriculum Assessment. Sarah was used to the older style of footnotes and using 'ibids' and 'op.cits.' in her earlier studying, but she is now happy with the Harvard system of referencing, finding it to be flexible and quick to use. Sarah has carried out her questionnaire and interviews with staff and has written up her research methods, data collection and analysis sections.

The tutor is pleased with Sarah's efforts which are now much more consistent and she feels that she may be able to submit by the completion deadline of 1st May. Sarah is now concentrating on producing her 'main findings' and then the 'conclusion and recommendations for future practice'. Her bibliography is not a problem as Sarah learnt to word process three years ago and she has stored the references, including those accessed via the internet, on disc and can rearrange them alphabetically at the touch of a button. She knows that she must use her appendix to support her findings and intends to include her questionnaire and interview schedule. Sarah does not yet fully realise that she also needs to produce an abstract of 200 words describing her dissertation structure, approach and findings. It would be a pity to rush this last section!

# Summary

- A **quotation** is useful in illustrating or supporting your point.

- **Short quotations** can be fitted into your text and be indicated by the use of 'single inverted commas'.

- **Longer quotations** need to be set apart from your own words, indented and single line spaced.

- When using only part of a quotation indicate the missing words by the use of **dots** . . .

- Make sure that your **references** are accurate and detailed.

- **Footnotes** provide the name of the author, title of publication, name of publisher, date of publication and page number.

- The **abbreviations** 'ibid.' and 'op.cit.' can be used when a reference has already been given in full.

- The **Harvard** system of referencing is now generally accepted in universities and is more flexible than the footnote system.

- In Harvard referencing you include the author's **name** and **date** of publication in the text.

- References used must be listed in a **bibliography** at the end of the assignment.

- Bibliographies should be **alphabetically** ordered and should provide details of the author's name, date of publication, title of publication, name of publisher and place of publication.

- An **appendix** can be used to provide supporting data for your assignment findings. Appendices must be numbered and referenced within the main body of your assignment.

- An **abstract** is a summary or synopsis of the main structure, approach and findings of your report or dissertation. The abstract should be completed with care.

- **Poor presentation** will affect your overall marks.

- Always leave generous **margins** at the top, bottom and sides of your assignment for tutor comments.

- Try to learn how to **type or word process** your assignment.

## Self-evaluation

1. Look back at your recent assignments and check the quotations. Did you indent and single line space any quotations that were longer than about twenty words?

2. Which system of referencing do you prefer and why?
   (a) Footnoting?
   (b) Harvard?

   Which system is favoured by your course?

3. How do you compile your list of references/ bibliography? Do you keep all of your references on separate pages so that you can arrange them in alphabetical order easily? Can you use your computer to store these references and order them?

4. What is your handwriting really like? Do you dot your 'i's accurately? Can you keyboard, or are you still learning this valuable skill? Critically analyse the layout and presentation of your last assignment according to the points given on pages 73–75.

# 8 Improving through reflection

Reflecting on your assignment writing skills is what this book has been about! The points covered in the chapters, the case studies, the self-evaluation questions – all have tried to engage you in 'learning through reflection'.

This penultimate chapter concentrates on the importance of **self-reflection** in recognising your strengths and identifying areas for further development. It also considers the value of tutor, colleague or family **feedback** on your assignments and how to use it constructively. The time to reflect on and to practise the skills of assignment writing has been clearly highlighted in the preceding chapters, but also deserves a final consideration. The chapter ends with a final **reflective profile** of the skills involved in good assignment writing.

## Recording your own progress

Reflecting on your learning through a **written evaluation** of your assignment writing skills is a useful way of recognising your strengths and identifying areas for further development.

### Keeping a portfolio

Many students nowadays keep a **professional development portfolio** in which they profile (or self-assess) their skills and in which they keep individual pieces of completed and assessed work as **evidence of achievement**. In relation to the assignment writing process there are many specific skills (*eg* bibliographic layout) and **generic** skills (*eg* information gathering) that you will have developed during your course. A skills profile helps you to identify which skills are 'highly developed' (a strength) and which skills 'need further development' (a relative weakness).

### Action

▪ Complete the skills (or competency) profile on pages 87–89 and self-assess your assignment writing skills or competences.

## The benefit of self-reflection

The benefit of self-reflection, using a skills profile, is that you can learn to become more self-aware and conscious of your present stage of development. Hopefully, the process of self-reflection will lead to increased **self-confidence** as you recognise your strengths and track your progress over a period of time. It is important to complete the self-assessments regularly in order to continually **review** your skills levels and to **set targets** for further development.

## Sharing your self-assessment

It is also important to share your self-assessments with your tutor in order to check out your perceptions. It may be possible that you are underestimating your present level of skills development or achievement. A tutorial session spent reviewing your work and using the reflective profile as a starting point for the discussion with your tutor can prove most enlightening. You may find that you have skills you did not realise you had!

## Using constructive feedback

**Tutor reflections** on your assignment writing skills are also an important source of learning and improvement. These reflections usually come in the form of written evaluations or assessments. In order to aid learning this tutor feedback needs to be both given and received constructively.

The following principles of giving and receiving constructive feedback have been provided for tutors and students in Higher Education. Read through these principles and consider:

- the feedback you receive from your tutor, and
- the way you receive the feedback.

## Giving and receiving constructive feedback

Feedback is information you give to people about their behaviour and its effect on you, how you feel towards them and what you want them to achieve.

Giving constructive feedback is therefore an important communication skill for tutors to use since it increases self-awareness, identifies options for alternative behaviour and this encourages development.

Both positive and negative feedback can be constructive or helpful if it is given skilfully since it identifies areas for continued or further improvement. Students give and receive feedback in a constructive way.

## The principles of giving constructive feedback

*Helpful feedback* – Tutors should take care to:

- *Be concrete and specific*: say exactly what the student is doing and focus on specific behaviour.
- *Refer to actions and behaviour*: say what the student is doing and what can be changed. Keep it impersonal.
- *Own the feedback*: make statements instead of general comments of praise or blame.
- *Be immediate*: be sure to give helpful feedback at the time it is needed. This is usually immediate but can also be at a planned time, a little later.
- *Be understood by the receiver*: make sure that the person receiving the feedback understands what you are saying. Use your active listening skills.

Students can be taken through these principles by the tutor as part of their ongoing development.

*Unhelpful feedback* – Tutors and students will give unhelpful feedback when they give criticism that:

- is vague or too general
- labels people
- is poorly timed

- *eg* 'I like your style'
- *eg* 'You're incompetent'
- delays in providing feedback lessen the likelihood of change.

*Plus . . .*

- **Helpful** positive feedback encourages the students to continue the behaviour that is successful.
- **Helpful** negative feedback allows the students to alter their actions, if they wish (you cannot force change).
- **Unhelpful** positive feedback is likely to make the receiver feel pleased or flattered but confused as to what s/he is doing right.
- **Unhelpful** negative feedback is likely to make the receiver feel angry, confused and upset. They will not know how to change their actions, or how to improve.

## Handling feedback constructively

Students and tutors can be encouraged to receive your feedback in a constructive way by adopting the following strategy:

- **Listen** – don't jump to your own defence immediately. Give yourself time to make sure you are clear about what is being said. Try repeating the evaluation to check out your understanding.
- **Decide** – whether the feedback is valid and helpful. You are entitled to reject the criticism, but remember that although feedback can be uncomfortable to hear, it is helpful to know how others see our behaviour.

- **Respond** – decide how to act as a result of the feedback: how to use the criticism to aid your personal and professional development.

- **Let go** – do not build up the criticism in your mind. It is often better to disclose how you feel about the feedback and the way in which it was given. Then let it go and move on.

Source: adapted from Acton, Kirkham and Smith (1991).

Tutors and students need to practise these skills of giving and receiving constructive feedback, in order to improve their skill level.

Reflect critically on the level of your and your tutor's skills development in the areas of:

(a) giving constructive feedback

(b) receiving constructive feedback.

Which level have you reached? See Figure 13.

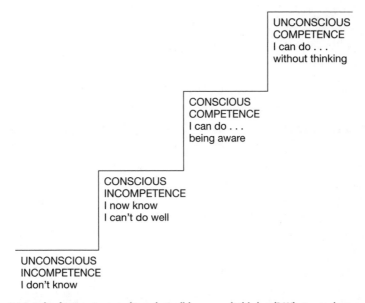

**Fig. 13** Levels of competence: why or how did you reach this level? What experiences helped you to develop these skills?

## Getting feedback from peers, friends and family

Besides tutor evaluations, valuable feedback can be gained from your peers, friends or family. As discussed in Chapter 6, you could ask a colleague, family member or friend to read your draft essay, report or dissertation chapter (all of it may be a little too much!). Ask them to give you constructive feedback on:

- the style of the assignment
- the structure of the assignment
- the logic of the argument
- the knowledge and understanding demonstrated
- the application to practice/personal interpretation.

All of this feedback – tutor comments and peer/family review – will help you to become more **self-aware** of your strengths and help you to identify those areas you need to further develop. **Targeting these weaknesses and then seeking out professional support** to help you to develop in these particular skill areas is the most effective way of managing your own learning. You will also become more confident in your own ability to improve. Support for this development can come from your tutor and also through supported self study using books like this.

*More than just 'marks'* – One final point about tutor feedback. Hopefully, your tutor will appreciate the need to provide constructive feedback in order to help you to develop in your assignment writing skills. This will entail her/him not simply giving you a 'mark', but recognising your strengths with a *positive comment* and identifying specifically your present weaknesses and then suggesting *ways of improving* your work.

- How meaningful is 'C+ – satisfactory'?

If your tutor's level of skills development in providing meaningful feedback is not high, then do practise the skills of constructive feedback yourself. Explain to the tutor that you need a **detailed** evaluation in order to improve your assignment writing skills.

■ Be assertive! Manage your own learning process as effectively as you can.

Remember, tutor assessment can never be totally objective. It is hoped that your tutor uses a criterion-referenced method of assessment (see Chapter 1). These criteria should be shared openly with you in order to help you to become aware of the knowledge, skills and conceptual understanding you need to demonstrate in your assignment. Tutors do sometimes get assessments wrong!

*Asking for the assessment to be reviewed* – You would be operating within your rights as a student if you were to ask the tutor to review the assessment given you. You need to be quite clear about your reasons for this request. That is, you need to understand the assessment criteria clearly to know how well your assignment fulfills these criteria. If you feel a mistake has been made, request a re-mark politely but firmly. Tutors often use a colleague for **double-marking** or **internal moderation**. Has your assignment been double-marked?

*Resolving misunderstandings* – Often a misunderstanding or disappointment about a mark can be explained in a tutorial session. Hopefully, your tutor will have provided you with detailed evaluative and constructive feedback that pinpoints where you went wrong and suggests ways of improving next time. *Talk to your tutor.*

# Time to reflect

In Chapter 2 the importance of managing your time effectively was stressed as an important skill in assignment writing. Certainly, more than one of our case study students has needed to develop good time management skills in order to succeed.

■ *Do you need to improve YOUR time management skills?*

## Learning requires time

- Time to reflect on your learning (self-reflection).
- Time to reflect on your drafted assignment (see Chapter 6).
- Time to reflect on your tutor's and others' feedback (learning through feedback).
- Time to practise the skills of assignment writing (drafting and redrafting).

*Plan and prioritise* – It is important to plan and prioritise your assignment writing, allocating quality time to the process of reflection and development.

- *When is your quality time for reflection? Do you think and work more effectively – in the mornings, afternoons, evenings or night?*

Remember, effective assignment writing is more about thinking and planning than actual writing. Thinking and planning need quality reflective time. Writing needs practice time.

- Never underestimate t*he amount of time* you need to complete an assignment to your satisfaction. This can be especially difficult to judge in an examination situation and needs to be rehearsed with care.
- Time spent *reflecting* in your learning is the most valuable use of your precious time and will reap rich dividends in further improvements.
- Time spent with *your tutor* in this reflection on your work should be doubly effective, as two heads are better than one and your tutor has expert advice to offer.
- Finally, time spent in *practising the skills* of assignment writing will be time well spent in your on-going professional development.

# A profile of assignment writing skills

Self-reflect against this profile and evidence your level of competence.

| Skills | Self-assessment Level of competence |
|---|---|
| *I understand the importance of assessment criteria in assignment writing*<br><br>– I understand the assessment criteria for the assignment/ course.<br><br>– I know that I must demonstrate knowledge of the subject, skills of research, application/interpretation of theory to practice, clear structure and accurate referencing. | |
| *I know myself as a learner*<br><br>– I know my preferred style of learning and its advantages and disadvantages.<br><br>– I have effective time management skills. | |
| *I understand the title question and answer it relevantly*<br><br>– I can analyse the key process and content words.<br><br>– I use a dictionary and *Roget's Thesaurus* to define their meaning.<br><br>– I can recognise open-ended, descriptive, analytical and argumentative questions. | |
| *I plan and take notes carefully*<br><br>– I use brainstorming to generate ideas.<br><br>– I use the internet to help my research.<br><br>– I use patterned notes and/or planning trees to provide an outline plan.<br><br>– I have an effective style of note-taking for my information gathering. | |

| Skills | Self-assessment Level of competence |
|---|---|
| *I know how to structure my rough draft* <br><br> – I use paragraphs, sub-headings and chapters to structure and signpost my assignment effectively. <br><br> – My paragraphs contain one main or sub-point. <br><br> – I use key sentences to explain the meaning of the paragraph. <br><br> – I use sub-headings wherever possible to signpost my structure. <br><br> – My introductions define the key words and state what will happen in the assignment. <br><br> – I use conclusions to pull the assignment together and I summarise the main points covered. | |
| *I know how to improve my style* <br><br> – I leave enough time to reflect on my drafted assignment and I edit it. <br><br> – I use an appropriate formal tone and I know my audience. <br><br> – I do not use slang, abbreviations, acronyms or contractions. <br><br> – I use simple straightforward language. <br><br> – I never plagiarise. <br><br> – I use transitions to help my assignment flow effectively. <br><br> – I use non-sexist language. | |
| *I know how to make an effective final presentation* <br><br> – I know how to present short and longer quotations. <br><br> – My references are detailed and accurate. <br><br> – I use the Harvard or footnoting system of referencing accurately. <br><br> – My bibliographies are complete and alphabetically ordered. <br><br> – I use an appendix to support my main findings wherever possible. | |

| Skills | Self-assessment Level of competence |
|---|---|
| – I complete my abstracts with care. | |
| – I can type or word process my assignment. | |
| – I leave generous margins at the top, bottom and sides. | |
| *I know how to improve through reflection* | |
| – I use tutor, peer and family feedback constructively to help me develop my skills. | |
| – I know that assignment writing requires reflection time and I prioritise this activity. | |
| – I use this profile regularly to review my competences. | |
| – I can recognise my strengths and identify my areas for further development. | |
| – I target my weaknesses and seek support for my further development. | |

## Summary

■ Keeping a **professional development portfolio** can help you to profile your skills and keep a record of your achievement in assignment writing.

■ Self assessing your skills using a **profile** can help you to recognise your strengths and identify areas for further development.

■ **Sharing your self-assessments** with your tutor can help to raise your self confidence.

■ Feedback from tutors and others can be helpful, but needs to be given and received *constructively*.

■ **Targeting** your areas of weakness and seeking **professional support** for further development are important.

■ Make sure that you understand the **assessment criteria** and that you can 'check' your tutor's assessment.

- Remember that *learning through reflection* takes time.
- *Practising* the skills of assignment writing takes **time**.

## Self-evaluation

1. Self-reflect against the skills profile on the previous pages and evidence your level of competence.

2. Analyse the feedback you have received to date from your tutor. Is it constructive? Have you received it constructively and acted on it? Do you ask your peer group for feedback on your assignment?

3. Do you prioritise reflection time? Do you allow yourself enough time to practise the skills of assignment writing?

# 9 Where are you now?

Our case studies have reached the end of their courses! They have completed and submitted all of their coursework assignments and Steve has just sat his 'A' level examinations. Where are they now?

---

**Case studies**

### How Steve has improved

Steve has developed his essay writing skills a good deal over the last year. His natural 'activist' style has been balanced by the development of a more 'reflective' approach to learning. Steve has also developed a keen desire to manage his time more effectively! He still juggles several balls in the air at the same time (cricket, football, rugby . . . ). However, his ability to receive tutor feedback constructively, and to act on it immediately, has saved him lots of time in the learning process.

Steve has just reflected on the skills profile (Chapter 8). He recognises that he has now developed a strength in the area of 'understanding the assessment criteria' and 'understanding and answering the question set'. When he thinks back to his first rushed sociology essay he feels slightly embarrassed! Steve now plans and structures his essays with care and his note-taking is improving. He has learned how to word process and finds this has helped his drafting and presentation skills. The compilation of bibliographies remains a source of difficulty: they never seem to be totally accurate. This area, plus note-taking, are identified by Steve as areas for further development, so he intends to target these skills particularly over the next year.

Steve's greatest strength lies in his ability to know himself, to recognise his weaknesses and then to identify specific areas for development and to seek practical support from his tutor. He found reading the chapter on 'how to plan your assignment' to be of great help.

▶

Steve has practised writing essays under fixed conditions in preparing for his examination. He realised that the skills of essay writing – particularly analysing the question and planning the structure – are vital in the examination. On the day, he made sure that he wrote the required four essays within the three hours allowed.

Steve has been conditionally accepted for a place on a HND PE and Leisure course. His essay writing skills came in very useful when he applied for the place, both in terms of planning his letter of application and in the presentation of it. Steve needs to pass both 'A' levels in order to take up the place. He is eagerly awaiting the results!

### Gill achieves a balanced professionalism

Gill started the year as a typical 'theorist', making lots of notes and references to other theorists' work, but not interpreting or applying them to her own practices. She has now learned to balance her predisposition to theory and logic with a more 'pragmatic' style which has helped her practical report writing skills. Gill's time management skills have much improved over the last year by her having consciously practised various strategies: for example, effective note-taking and using and storing references, especially on her new personal computer (PC).

Gill has enjoyed her management course. Her tutor has been good at giving 'constructive feedback' on specific areas of further development. She needed to improve her application of the theory to practice, to develop confidence in conducting interviews and questionnaires with colleagues, and in using this data effectively in her findings. Gill can now produce a very effective management report in a much shorter length of time than her first effort! She has worked hard and has practised the skills of report writing throughout the year.

Gill has now gained in overall self-confidence. She can talk more easily with people she does not know well. Her skills profile reveals an increased self-awareness of her strengths, particularly in 'learning through reflection', 'analysis of the question', 'planning', 'structuring' and 'understanding the assessment criteria'. She feels that she has learned a lot about management and wants to progress to the advanced stage of the management diploma if her grades are good enough. Gill has set as her targets for development: 'knowing how to improve your style', particularly the 'use of simple and straightforward language' and the 'use of transitions' to aid the flow of her writing.

Gill's overall result in the management course is due out very soon!

## Sarah's greater maturity

Sarah has surprised herself and her tutor by submitting her dissertation on time! Sarah's natural 'reflector' style of learning was helpful in coming up with creative ideas during her data collection period and she could see several attractive ways of interpreting this data. She needed, however, to develop a more 'activist' and 'pragmatic' style of working in order to actually get started on the research project!

Luckily her tutor spotted this potential weakness early on and provided the necessary guidance and support to keep her 'feet on the ground'. Sarah's creative and imaginative skills have therefore been 'controlled' over the year in favour of a more logical, planned and structured approach to dissertation writing. A big turning point in her skills development came when her tutor helped her to generate an outline plan for 'Teacher Stress and National Curriculum assessment'. Sarah found this most helpful, particularly in the literature review and data analysis chapters of the dissertation. She now uses plans more frequently in her daily life and finds them a most effective time management strategy.

Sarah is good at self-reflection; her skills profile reveals clear strengths in the area of 'allocating reflection time to the process of learning'. She feels that she has spent many hours reflecting on her research during this dissertation year (her children thought she was day dreaming!). She knows that this reflection time has helped her to improve the quality of her data analysis and interpretation and she has been able to edit her drafted chapters to her satisfaction.

Sarah knows that she must continue to target and practise the skills of 'planning', 'structuring', and in particular 'the pulling together of her main points into a pertinent conclusion'. She hopes that she has managed to demonstrate these skills satisfactorily in her dissertation, in the end. Sarah did produce a rather hurried 'abstract' about an hour before handing in her dissertation. She is still targeting time management as an area for ongoing professional development.

Sarah's MA results are due out shortly!

Our three case studies have reflected against the skills profile on pages 87–89 and have targeted certain areas for their further development.

**Steve**

| Target | Action plan |
| --- | --- |
| | How will you achieve your target? What help do you need? |
| ■ To make sure that my bibliographies are complete and alphabetically ordered. | *Learn how to use IT more effectively.* |
| ■ To improve the effectiveness of my note-taking/information gathering. | *Try different strategies of note-taking. Read a chapter/book on taking notes effectively.* |

**Gill**

| Target | Action plan |
| --- | --- |
| ■ To use more simple and straightforward language in reports. | *Study good management reports and practise the skills of clarity.* |
| ■ To use transitions more effectively to aid the flow of my writing. | *Use transitions to link my paragraphs. Practise this skill.* |

**Sarah**

| Target | Action plan |
| --- | --- |
| ■ To continue to plan with care. | *Use planning techniques – eg planning trees.* |
| ■ To structure my writing. | *Use sub-headings more frequently.* |
| ■ To use conclusions effectively. | *Summarise my main points. Practise this skill. Ask colleagues to check it for me with care.* |

# And how about you?

■ What was the result of your skills profile? What specific targets did you set? How will you achieve your target? What help do you need?

■ Please complete your own target-setting/action-planning pro-forma, below.

| Target | Action plan |
|---|---|
| | How will you achieve your target? What help do you need? |
| ■ To... | |

# Conclusion

Our case studies have just received their results:

■ Steve has passed both 'A' levels and is going to start his HND course in September. He celebrates his achievement at the Rugby Club!

- Gill has received a commendation for her management course and her tutors want her to progress to the advanced course in September. Her company gives her a pay rise in recognition of her achievement!

- Sarah has passed her MA. She feels at a bit of a loose end now and has volunteered to research and write an assessment policy document for school. She intends to apply for Head of Key Stage posts immediately!

'Our case studies are continuing with their assignment writing skills development.' ***ARE YOU?***

# Glossary

**Abstract.** A summary or synopsis of the completed report or dissertation.

**Appendix.** Material at the back of the assignment, used to provide supporting data.

**Assignment.** An investigative research resulting in a piece of writing *eg* essay, report, dissertation.

**Assessment criteria.** The knowledge, skills and understanding you need to demonstrate in your assignment.

**Audience.** The receivers of your assignment.

**Bibliography.** A complete list of all quotations and references included in the assignment.

**Brainstorming.** An activity to generate ideas and material for the assignment.

**Constructive feedback.** Evaluations from tutors and others helping you to improve.

**Dissertation.** Major written assignments undertaken towards the end of diploma, degree, Masters and PhD courses.

**Essay.** A flowing piece of writing, answering the title question set and which has an introduction, main body and conclusion.

**Key sentence.** The sentence in the paragraph explaining the main point of the paragraph.

**Key words.** Those words that indicate the important criteria or substance of a sentence.

**Learning style.** Preferred ways of working and studying.

**Managing time.** Analysing and improving your use of time to improve effectiveness.

**Paragraph.** An organising device for text which usually has one main point.

**Patterned notes.** An outline or detailed planning technique.

**Planning tree.** An outline or detailed planning technique.

**Professional development portfolio.** A record of the skills achieved, targets set and evidence of achievement.

**Project report.** A written evaluative report on an activity undertaken which has a clear structure.

**Quotations.** The use of someone else's words directly.

**References.** Providing the source of your quotations and references for the reader.

**Sub-heading.** An organising device or signpost for the reader.

**Transitions.** Linking words or phrases which give flow to a piece of writing.

# Further Reading

*Critical Thinking for Students*, Roy van den Brink-Budgen, 4th edn (How To Books, 2010).

*Essay to Write?* Brendan Hennessy (How To Books, 2002).

*A Guide to Learning Independently*, L. A. Marshall and F. Rowland, 3rd edn (Open University Press, 1998).

*How to Pass Your Exams*, Mike Evans (How To Books, 2009).

*How to Write Coursework and Exam Essays*, Brendan Hennessy, 6th edn (How To Books, 2010).

*How To Write Essays*, R. Lewis (Collins, 1993).

*Improve Your Punctuation and Grammar*, Marion Field, 3rd edn (How To Books, 2009).

*Improve Your Written English*, Marion Field, 5th edn (How To Books, 2009).

*The Manual of Learning Styles*, P. Honey and A. Mumford, 2nd edn (Honey, 1986).

*Open Teaching Tool Kit – Writing Skills* (Open University Press, 1991).

*Oxford Dictionary* (Oxford University Press, 1997).

*Quick Solutions to Common Errors in English*, Angela Burt, 4th edn (How To Books, 2009).

*Study and Learn*, S. Asham and A. George (Heinemann, 1982).

*Studying for a Degree*, P. Dunleavy (Macmillan, 1980).

*Writing Your Dissertation*, Derek Swetnam, 3rd edn (How To Books, 2000).

Further Reading

# Index

# Some other titles from How To Books

## Improve Your Punctuation and Grammar

Master the essentials of the English language and write with greater confidence

*Marion Field*

> 'An invaluable guide...after reading this book, you will never again find yourself using a comma instead of a semi-colon.' – *London Evening Standard*

> 'I realised for the first time that grammar is actually fascinating... you are given the facts in plain English – no waffle, no padding, just the details you really need...a fascinating and readable book.' – *Writing Magazine*

> 'This book does exactly what it says on the front cover: it helps you master the basics of the English language and write with greater confidence and clarity.' – *MS London*

ISBN 978-1-84528--329-2

## Introduction To Research Methods

Dr Catherine Dawson

'I would certainly recommend this book to others. I found it extremely informative and will refer to it often.' A reader, UK

'It is compact, practical, easy to read and well laid out. If every student kept a copy by him/her during the course of the research, as a quick guide, it would certainly assist methodology and results.' – *Training Journal*

ISBN 978-1-84528-367-4

## Your Phd Companion

Stephen Marshall & Nick Green

'This comprehensive book provides advice on embarking on and completing a PhD, tales of student life and anecdotes about the experiences of some famous PhD students, including Einstein.' – *The Independent*

'… a most excellent find! … honest and uncompromising. Apart from hair-tearing PhD students, I'd also recommend the book to prospective PhD students.' Reader review

ISBN 978-1-84528-392-6

# How to Write Coursework and Exam Essays

An accessible guide to developing the skills needed to excel in written work and exams

*Brendan Hennessey*

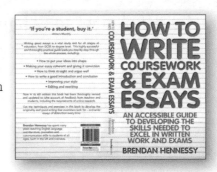

'There is a lot of good sense in this book.' *Times Educational Supplement*

'If you're a student, buy it.' *Writer's Monthly*

Writing good essays is a vital study skill for all stages of education, from GCSE to degree level. This highly successful and thoroughly practical guide leads you step-by-step through the whole process, including:

- How to put your ideas into shape
- Making your essay coherent and giving it conviction
- How to think straight and argue well
- How to write a good introduction and conclusion
- Improving your style
- Editing and rewriting

Now in its 6th edition this book has been thoroughly revised and updated to take account of feedback from teachers and students, including the requirements of online research.

Use the techniques and exercises in this book to develop the originality and good writing that examiners look for – and write essays of distinction every time.

Now in a thoroughly revised and updated 6th edition

**Brendan Hennessy** has spent many years teaching English language and literature, journalism, and communication skills to students of all ages both in the UK and overseas.

ISBN 978-1-84528-440-4

## Quick Solutions to Common Errors in English

An A-Z guide to spelling, punctuation and grammar

*Angela Burt*

'You will never doubt your written English again.' – *Evening Standard*

'A very useful tool...could easily fill that hole on your bookshelf.' – *Irish Independent*

'...straightforward and accessible handbook for anyone who ever has a query about correct English – and that's all of us.' – *Freelance News*

ISBN 978-1-84528-361-2


## Improve Your Written English

Master the essentials of grammar, punctuation and spelling and write with greater confidence

*Marion Field*

'If your written English is letting you down, do something about it. This book is recommended.' – Evening Standard

'This book is a gem. If you never buy another reference book, buy this one!' – *Writers' Express*

ISBN 978-1-84528-331-5

# The Complete Study Skills Guide

A practical guide for all students who want to know how to learn
*Dr Catherine Dawson*

Successful study is dependent on effective study skills. Yet many students are never taught how to study, and many are anxious about their ability to develop the necessary skills required to complete their course.

All students can learn how to study. It is not a skill reserved for the select few. With a little information, guidance and advice all students can discover how to study and improve the marks on their course.

This book is aimed at all students who wish to improve their study skills at almost every level, including college and university students, adult learners, and students on correspondence and distance learning courses.

It provides a user-friendly, practical guide to study skills, including information on:

- preparing for, taking and passing examinations
- how to read for study efficiently and effectively
- how to hypothesise, theorise, critique and analyse
- improving your mathematical and scientific skills
- completing projects and assignments
- how to get the most out of lectures, tutorials, classes and seminars
- time management, organising yourself and building motivation
- ways you can improve your marks

Quotations, case studies, exercises and useful tips are also included, along with information about study skills websites, software and online tools.

For over twenty-five years, **Dr Catherine Dawson** has been a researcher specialising in educational research, and a tutor working with college and university students. She has written extensively for both academic journals and popular magazines and is passionate about providing information to help students succeed on their courses.

ISBN 978-1-84528-445-9

# How To Speed Read

*Gordon Wainwright*

> 'Purely practical and aims to help you in the professional environment.' *The Times*

In today's information-laden and time-constrained world we are required to digest

an increasing amount of written and printed material. Most people in their capacity as student, job seeker, employee or leisure reader, want to be able to deal with their daily reading faster and recall it effectively.

This book gives you the means to do just that by:

- Finding the techniques for improvement that work best for you
- Providing methods for increasing retention and recall
- Promoting flexibility – the key to reading efficiently
- Offering techniques for developing skim-reading
- Highlighting problem areas and suggesting ways of addressing them

This book contains exercises to facilitate your development and assess your results throughout, ensuring that you come away reading faster and recalling more.

ISBN 978-1-84528-428-2

## How To Pass Your Exams

Proven Techniques for any exam that will guarantee success

*Mike Evans*

> "Brisk, shrewd and full of useful tips. An excellent book." *The Daily Telegraph*

> 'The absolute bible for any one taking any exam at any level.' *Reader, UK*

Whatever exams you're taking, this book really will make a big difference to your performance – at professional or academic level; Master's or GCSE; A level, essay or multiple choice.

Many hard working, intelligent people still fail their exams through lack of confidence or poor exam technique. At least fifty per cent of a candidate's chances are down to:

- Taking the right attitude into the exam
- Using simple but very effective techniques in the exam itself
- Approaching your course of study in the right way

These factors are your guarantee of success. They are easy to learn and proven beyond doubt. They will also boost your confidence so that you arrive in the exam room both ready and able to succeed.

**Mike Evans** has never failed an exam. He now teaches other people how to pass exams and regularly achieves one hundred per cent pass rates in his classes. He holds a Master's Degree in Business Administration; is an Accountant, a Fellow of the Institute of Management, a Master Practitioner of Neuro-Linguistic Programming, a qualified pilot and a successful lecturer.

> 'This book offers simple tools, insights and approaches that will inspire confidence and prepare you (or your students) for examination success.' Focus on Business Education

ISBN 978-1-84528-444-2

# Writing Your Dissertation

The bestselling guide to planning, preparing and presenting first-class work

*Derek Swetnam*

> The chapters are relevant and helpful and contain information such as some of the most common spelling mistakes. This book is a great basic start.' – Amazon Reader Review

> 'This book has been a lifesaver! Half way through a dissertation I suddenly realised that I was drifting aimlessly. This book gave me guidance and helped me to structure my dissertation plan when I needed it most. I would definitely recommend it to others!' – Amazon Reader Review

ISBN 978-1-85703-662-6

How To Books are available through all good bookshops, or you can order direct from us through Grantham Book Services.

Tel: +44 (0)1476 541080
Fax: +44 (0)1476 541061
Email: orders@gbs.tbs-ltd.co.uk

Or via our website
**www.howtobooks.co.uk**

To order via any of these methods please quote the title(s) of the book(s) and your credit card number together with its expiry date.

For further information about our books and catalogue, please contact:

How To Books
Spring Hill House
Spring Hill Road
Begbroke
Oxford
OX5 1RX

Visit our web site at
**www.howtobooks.co.uk**

Or you can contact us by email at info@howtobooks.co.uk